access to sociology

EDUCATION, TRAINING
and POLICY

Paul Selfe

Series Editor: Paul Selfe

Withdrawn

Hodder & Stoughton

A MEMBER OF THE HODDER HEADLINE GROUP

DEDICATION

To Hilary and Howard.

Orders: please contact Bookpoint Ltd, 39 Milton Park, Abingdon, Oxon OX14 4TD.
Telephone: (44) 01235 400414, Fax: (44) 01235 400454. Lines are open from 9.00–6.00,
Monday to Saturday, with a 24 hour message answering service.
Email address: orders@bookpoint.cu.uk

A catalogue record for this title is available from The British Library

ISBN 0 340 78033 9

First published 2000
Impression number 10   9   8   7   6   5   4   3   2   1
Year   2005   2004   2003   2002   2001   2000

Cover photo by Jeremy Pardoe

Typeset by Transet Limited, Coventry, England.
Printed in Great Britain for Hodder & Stoughton Educational, a division of
Hodder Headline plc, 338 Euston Road, London NW1 3BH by Redwood Books,
Trowbridge, Wilts.

CONTENTS

ACKNOWLEDGEMENTS

I am deeply grateful to Lorna, and my daughters, Jess and Amy for their constant support and help at all times throughout the writing of this book and during the project as a whole. Their enthusiasm and interest has been a great encouragement to me. I have also been given invaluable assistance in the editorial and production work of Luke Hacker, Chris Loades and their colleagues at Hodder and Stoughton, who have kept the work on this book, and others in the series on line. They have always provided constructive suggestions and helpful guidance. There have been moments of crisis which they have always managed to resolve. I thank, too, Elizabeth Tribe at whose suggestion the series began, for her support. I am also greatly indebted to other authors in the series for their thoroughly professional approach in the writing of their books. It has been a great pleasure to work with them all. The photographs in this book, by Jeremy Pardoe, have been used with the permission of David Noon, Headmaster of Weobley High School, Herefordshire. I am most appreciative of their co-operation in providing these. Thanks also to Diana Goddard.

1

INTRODUCTION

HOW TO USE THE BOOK

EACH CHAPTER IN this book examines one or more of the central debates relating to sociology of education. The text is devised for readers with little or no background knowledge in the subject, and there are Study Points and Activities throughout to encourage a consideration of the issues raised. You are advised to make use of these and answer them either on paper or in group discussion, a particularly fruitful way of learning; they will assist you to develop the skills of interpretation, analysis and evaluation. There are many ways of preparing for an exam, but a thorough understanding of the material is obviously crucial.

Each chapter is structured to give a clear understanding of the authors, concepts and issues that you need to know about. To assist understanding and facilitate later revision it is often helpful to make short notes.

MAKING NOTES FROM THE BOOK

These should be short, relevant and complete.

- Include a page number
- Write the notes in your own words.
- They should make clear sense for later reference.

You could try two systems to record points, which show how they are linked to an overall argument or theory. One can take the form of linear notes, and the other a pattern or diagram with arrows showing the way they relate together. A combination of both may be appropriate. Note-making, whether from a speaker, a video, audio tape or from a book, is a skill which requires practice. Devise a scheme which you use in a consistent way, using coloured pens.

Linear notes

- Bold headings establish key points: names, theories and concepts.
- Subheadings indicate details of relevant issues.
- A few numbered points list related arguments.

Diagrams

- Use a large blank sheet of paper and write a key idea in the centre.
- Make links between this and related issues.
- Show also the connections between sub-issues which share features in common.

Both systems have their advantages and disadvantages, and may take some time to perfect. Linear notes can be little more than a copy of what is already in a book and patterned notes can be confusing. But if you practise the skill, they can reduce material efficiently and concisely, becoming invaluable for revision. Diagrammatic notes may be very useful for those with a strong visual memory and provide a clear overview of a whole issue, showing patterns of interconnection. The introduction of helpful drawings or a touch of humour into the format is often a good way to facilitate the recall of names, research studies and complex concepts. Produce effective evaluation notes by highlighting or underlining your text in different pens; you could even use symbols or icons in the margins to depict strengths or weaknesses.

HOW TO FOCUS ON KEY ISSUES

Look for key authors, theories, concepts and issues, which are tabulated at the start of each chapter. The names of sociologists are important because they act as the hook on which you can hang related ideas, especially theories and research details. Their view may also be necessary with reference to coursework projects, or as sources for more detail. Definitions of terms and concepts are vital because you must become familiar with the language of sociology. There are excellent dictionaries of sociology available and it is important to have access to one. When reading in preparation for a written question, or to feel confident that you have covered the ground, it may be useful to:

- Make summary diagrams which are legible and understandable for future reference.
- Decide on your interpretations of the points made. Do you tend to agree or disagree with the position they represent?
- Discuss the ideas raised with someone else. Encourage them to ask you probing questions. This will reveal the extent of your understanding.
- Decide where you stand in relation to issues raised; can you study the topic in a detached way?

Make and keep **Key Concept Cards**, as shown below.

Hidden curriculum

Key idea: a term used by sociologists to describe all the other things learnt during schooling apart from the official curriculum. It is the power of the unofficial three Rs: rules, regulations and routine, to influence patterns of behaviour. These rules must be learnt by pupils to cope with everyday schooling.

Among the many writers who use the term are:
Meighan, R.; Jackson, P.; Becker, H.

Points of criticism: it is an ambiguous concept and hard to define with precision. But it does have explanatory powers.

Syllabus area: sociological theories of education including factors affecting performance.

EXAMINATION ADVICE

To develop an effective method of writing, answers should be:

- **Sociological:** use the language and research findings of sociologists; do not use anecdotal opinion gathered from people not involved in sociology to support arguments.
- **Adequate in length:** enough is written to obtain the marks available.
- **Interconnected** with other parts of the syllabus (such as stratification, gender, ethnicity).
- **Logical:** the answer follows from the relevant evidence.
- **Balanced:** arguments and counter arguments are weighed; references are suitable.
- **Accurate:** reliable data is obtained from many sources.

The three skill areas on page 3 should be demonstrated, so that the question is answered effectively. Further suggestions are made at the end of each chapter.

In displaying knowledge, the student is not necessarily also demonstrating interpretation.

The skill of evaluation is a very important one. It means that the strengths and weaknesses of evidence are assessed and an overall judgement about its value is made.

COURSEWORK ADVICE

Coursework provides an opportunity to carry out a study using primary and/or secondary data to investigate an issue of sociological interest. It must address theoretical issues and be based on one or more areas of the syllabus being studied. The suggestions included at the end of each chapter may be adapted or used to generate further ideas. But, before you begin, always take time to plan your intended research. Final decisions must be agreed with a teacher or tutor.

MAKING A PLAN

1 Read and make notes from articles describing research projects in journals.
2 Have a clear aim in mind; choose an issue that interests you and is within your ability.
3 Decide more precisely what you want to know; establish a simple hypothesis to test.
4 Select a range of possible methods; consider both quantitative and qualitative.
5 Decide on a range of possible sources of information.
6 List the people from whom you can seek help, perhaps including a statistician.

WRITING THE PROJECT

1 Seek frequent advice from a teacher or tutor.
2 Check the weighting for different objectives in the marking scheme.
3 Keep clear notes throughout, including new ideas and any problems that arise.
4 Limit its length (maximum 5,000 words).

2

IDEOLOGY AND EDUCATION

Introduction

THIS CHAPTER EXAMINES the ways in which the educational system in England and Wales has been influenced by changing political ideologies. It is difficult to appreciate the impact of these influences without taking account of the ideological values of the politicians who put them in place. These shaped the types of schools which were established, the kinds of curriculum taught in them, the subsequent changes over time, as well as the policies considered appropriate.

Table 1: *Key Authors, Concepts and Issues in this chapter*		
KEY AUTHORS	KEY CONCEPTS	KEY ISSUES
Thompson Halsey	Ideology and political values Ideology and education	Definition and relevance Every party emphasises a different ideological theme
Weber	Ideology and power	Significance of ideology for understanding power and authority in society
Marx	Ideology and false consciousness	Significance of ideology as a means of deluding people
Durkheim	Ideology and social stability	Significance of ideology as a social cement
Erikson	Moral order	Education as a source of social cohesion

Usher and Edwards	Postmodernism	Education can not be a source of social engineering in post-modern times
Hayek	Inequality	Education inevitably promotes inequality
Crossland	Equality	Education should promote equality
Chitty	Educational opportunity	Variations between the main political parties relate to their ideological values
Leadbeater	New Right	Justification for innovative and varied forms of schooling

THE SIGNIFICANCE OF IDEOLOGY

Thompson (*Beliefs and Ideology* 1986) has said that 'Ideologies are beliefs which have implications for people's perception of their position in society and the nature of society.' People may share different types of ideological belief in relation to politics, religion, class, gender, ethnicity and education, providing a sense of identity and community. Sociologists generally treat the concept as one which describes a set of interlocked ideas about society which are held by a group (and which may vary, for example, between those who are *Telegraph* and those who are *Guardian* readers). Ideologies provide competing belief systems by which people make sense of the world. **Halsey** (1986) said that in Britain 'ideologically, national histories of education seem to have echoed … the themes of liberty, equality and fraternity.' These themes have been taken up by different political parties, which have given emphasis to one or other of them in their policies.

THE STRUCTURE OF EDUCATION IN ENGLAND AND WALES

The historical background in which education has developed in Britain has resulted in a complex structure in which religious and elitist attitudes and independent and state agencies have played significant parts. The educational system is controlled by the party which wins the election; invariably they inherit a well established structure, which even though they may be opposed ideologically to some aspects, it is often very difficult to reverse. Some power is held by Local Education Authorities; those in Conservative areas are able to retain grammar schools, develop city technology colleges and other systems which fit closely with underlying Conservative ideology. Those in Labour held authorities ensure that the comprehensive system is effective.

The independent sector is deeply entrenched and although they involve only a minority of the school population (less than 8 per cent of children aged 5–15) they have become part of the educational landscape. In power, the Labour Party tends only to limit the opportunities they have of attracting pupils to them. Total abolition is considered too politically difficult. There have been changes in structure as ideological values have shifted. These become subject to debate and compromise, as governments seek to put into place policies based on underlying party values, as well as seeking to retain the support of the majority of the electorate.

Table 2:

KEY ISSUES IN EDUCATION POLCY IN THE TWENTIETH CENTURY (ENGLAND & WALES)

1902	Balfour's Education Act	Established Local Education Authorities to provide secondary education to age 13	Conservatives
1907		School medical inspections; school meal	Liberals
1918	Fisher's Education Act	More able pupils given vocational training. Leaving age 14	Liberals
1926	Hadow Report	Introduced 11+ and concept of primary and secondary education	Conservatives
1938	Spens Report	Advocated tripartite system: Grammar Secondary Modern; Technical schools	
1943	Norwood Report	Special curricula to suite children of different abilities	Coalition (Butler a Conservative)
1944	Butler's Education Act	Implemented Hadow and Spens; 146 LEAs to produce a system of education suited to age, aptitude and ability of each child. Three stages of education: Primary, Secondary and Further. Leaving age 15	
1946	Circular 147	Introduced Comprehensive Schools: "the secondary education of all children in a given area without organisation on three sides"	Labour

1959	Crowther Report	Advocated broadening scientific education; numbers in full time education to be doubled	Conservatives
1964	Newsome Report	Concerned with children of average or less than average ability. Attacked the 11+.	Labour
1967	Plowden Report	Concerned with need for improvements in primary education. Advocated abolition of 11+.	Labour
1972		School leaving age 16	Labour
1976	James Callaghan's Ruskin College speech	He called for new educational priorities in relation to standards	Labour
1976	Education Act	LEAs compelled to draw up plans for comprehensive schools (still lacking in some Conservative dominated areas)	Labour
1979–1997	The New Vocationalism	A range of new policies were introduced to promote more business-oriented curriculum and many new qualifications. See Ch. 10	Conservatives
1988	Education Reform Act	See Ch. 10.	
1993	Education Act	Further Education Colleges to become self-governing. Funding based on student numbers. Polytechnics become universities.	Conservatives
1997	New Labour's Educational agenda	See page 16	Labour

THE SOCIOLOGICAL INTERPRETATIONS OF IDEOLOGY

An ideology of education describes a set of beliefs which a group holds about the way an educational system should be organised; its structure, functions and methods. There are both theoretical and practical implications.

A WEBERIAN VIEW OF IDEOLOGY

• Sociology deals with the relations of domination and power among groups, organisations and institutions which are subject to different values and norms. The ideologies they produce and which sustain them are therefore of interest to sociologists since they are of significance in the maintenance and transformation of power in society.

The significance for education
Weber was interested in the problem of how order and harmony could be achieved in a society in which traditional religious values were declining. Well-organized schools, with competitive examinations, specialization, and chains of command were all justified. Such educational institutions and structures were important because they assisted in the promotion of several goals, which include the recognition of :

• Rational structures which are bureaucratic and efficient (also in evidence in the world of work in an efficient capitalist society).
• Reciprocal social behaviour as the basis of sound social relations. For Weber 'a social relation is present where individuals base their behaviour on the expected behaviour of others.'
• The substitution of ancient custom by planned goal oriented behaviour.
• The recognition of legitimate authority (the teacher); so that when in employment there will be acceptance of work-related rules.
• The recognition of the routes to status and power through endeavour.

Points of evaluation
(i)   This perspective leads to a liberal, meritocratic view of education, where the aim is to benefit both the individual, by encouraging goals, self interest and achievement, and the state, for which the objectives are efficiency and well ordered rational systems, based on expertise. A highly qualified citizen would enable the state to function more effectively. A plurality of institutions and methods can be justified according to local needs and demands.
(ii) Critics point out that to emphasise the importance of high level qualifications ensures that major inequalities will remain in the system. Furthermore, rational bureaucratic systems do not always benefit the individual, whose special needs and interests may not be recognized quickly. There remain many problems in establishing a truly meritocratic system that does not have class factors underpinning it.

MARXIST VIEW OF IDEOLOGY

This perspective argues that ideology refers to the beliefs which relate to the special interests of different classes. These arise from the economic system which forms the basis of society and from which different class interests develop. A Marxist analysis emphasises the need for changes in social organisations. It examines:

• The ways in which people are socially divided.
• How these divisions are supported by the educational structures.
• Why people remain deluded about the systems that oppress them and suffer false consciousness.

The significance for education

From this critical point of view:

- The educational structure is closely associated with existing political and economic systems. Children are taught virtues which do not threaten the equilibrium of the economic system, with the promise of success if they are sufficiently conforming. It is one of the ideological state apparatuses which is used as a means of preventing revolutionary movements.
- The social system is conflict ridden; power is unequally distributed; the poorest sector will accept it without question, until they are politicised.
- To label an issue or a child as 'a problem' helps diffuse responsibility for its existence. It is convenient for the ruling elite to have their definition of 'a problem' and its causes, accepted, since they can provide the solution, in the use of professional experts who aspire to high status and class, who do not affect the distribution of wealth or power.

Points of evaluation

(i)   The concern is about the effects of class division and the resulting inequalities. Major social reforms are advocated rather than a tinkering with the education system.

(ii) Critics of this view argue that these differences have become less significant in recent years, with more working-class children achieving academic successes.

DURKHEIM'S VIEW OF IDEOLOGY

Durkheim saw a shared ideology as the cement that helps to hold a society together. To achieve social order and stability people must be socialised to see the value of maintaining their institutions and belief systems. This was why it was important to have a shared religion with which people could identify. Every institution, including that of education, requires the use of special symbols, rituals and ceremonies to reinforce the sense of identification and commitment to the society. These help people to know who they are and how they relate to their society. The symbols include all those things that help provide their identity. Each day in school, children may meet for an assembly, say prayers, hear of the School's successes, all of which are intended to make them feel a member of their school community or wider society. It is these symbolic structures which constitute 'ideological communities'. Sociologists examine the symbols and to see how they work and what happens if some are abandoned.

The significance for education

Functionalist theory emphasises the role education plays in helping to establish an ideological community, shared beliefs about what constitutes the good society and the moral life, its protection and promotion. **Durkheim** said: 'it is obvious that all education consists of a continual effort to impose upon the child ways of seeing, thinking and acting which he himself would not have arrived at spontaneously.'

Its object is 'to create a social being'. These values become absorbed into the philosophies of political parties, who in a democratic society, fight for power at specified intervals.

This view implies that:

- Since there are pluralistic values in society, different types of school are necessary.

- Children who are disruptive (non-conformist or aberrant in behaviour) have been badly socialised; or they may be subject to the effects of weaknesses in society in which social disorganization results in deviance. For example, long-term unemployment may undermine family stability. They may require specialist treatment.

- Underachievement in school is the result of individual problems or a weakness in the school organisation. Measures are justified to restore balance and order.

Points of evaluation
(i)   Since the emphasis is on the search for order, these 'problems' are treated as if they are non-political, non-sociological and non-ideological. It presents a conservative view that favours the status quo.

(ii) **Thompson** (1986) says the functionalist analysis of Durkheim and that of certain Marxists share many features in common. They each see ideologies as systems of representations, composed of concepts, ideas, myths or images, in which people live out what they take to be the real relationships of their lives (their affections, identities, moralities) in terms of the real conditions of existence.

(iii) **Erikson** (1966) argued that a society requires moral order and must establish moral boundaries for people to accept. Educational systems can be used for this end, to unite the members of the society more closely together and reinforce the dominant ideology which cemented them in a cohesive unit.

Activity

Consider this statement made by the US Supreme Court in 1940 and answer the questions:

'National unity is the basis of national security ... the ultimate foundation of a free society is the binding tie of cohesive sentiment. We live by symbols. The flag is the symbol of our national unity, transcending all internal differences.'

Questions:

1. Suggest ways in which this statement illustrates Durkheim's view of the significance of symbols and rituals in maintaining traditional social solidarity in a society.
2. Suggest some of the symbols used to unite members of a school.

A POSTMODERN VIEW OF IDEOLOGIES

There is a rejection of classical theories about the ways that historical or economic forces influence development and change. There are many ideas which flow through societies, especially when the mass media are operating on a global scale, so that events are seen in real time wherever they occur and information is available in ever-increasing amounts through new technologies. Even identities may not be created (or constrained) through social class background, their religious or school affiliation, gender or ethnic membership. In a postmodern world people can choose from a range of options. There are said to be no longer any certainties or moral absolutes. Group identities, such as those of belonging to a particular class become less significant and so undermine the possibility of cohesive group ideologies.

Significance for education

Usher and Edwards (Postmodernism and Education, 1994) make the point that in the postmodern world, education can not be seen as having particular goals to achieve (such as truth, enlightenment, emancipation). Education becomes much more diverse in terms of structure, curricula, methods and participation. It takes its cue from diverse cultural contexts. 'The age old question of whether education is to merely reproduce the social order or is to be the vehicle for social change could no longer be answered definitively either way. Education can no longer be seen as part of a predictable reality and therefore can neither control nor be controlled.'

Therefore, it could neither be used as an instrument of social engineering nor as a means of reproducing society.

Points of evaluation

Much of the speculation is interesting and does provide a new approach to the analysis of what education may be like in the future. It points to an end of ideology, when education is free from the control of policy-makers who have certain goals in mind, either those of promoting liberty or equality, in the context of social progress. Every experience becomes educational and it could be that formal education loses any distinctive role and there are no responsibilities for standards or goals.

Study point
The Open University has no special building, times of lectures, or face-to-face meetings between students and those who devise the courses. How might these facts be interpreted from a postmodern point of view?

POLITICAL IDEOLOGIES AND EDUCATION

CONSERVATIVE IDEOLOGY

This represents the views that the best of the past should be conserved, especially such institutions as the monarchy and the church; grammar schools, and the capitalist free market economy must be preserved at all costs. Among the key beliefs of conservatism are those of 'freedom of choice', 'individualism' and 'rights'. The view would be that people must be as free as possible to pursue their individual interests, aims and goals and bear the consequences of their actions, should they meet problems. The presentation of egalitarian policies of the Labour Party are seen as a threat to them. Freedom and individualism require inequalities in wealth. The ability of the Conservative government after 1979 to impose their ideological values resulted from their successes in three consecutive general elections. Various conservative theorists have suggested that the ideology justifies:

- Selection in schools according to ability and income.
- The emphasis on selection; grammar schools and private schools.
- Hostility to the comprehensive principle.
- Concepts of individual failure through personal weaknesses.
- The inevitability and necessity of inequality. **Hayek** (1960) welcomed 'the degree of inequality that the USA had achieved as wholly admirable'.
- Limited government intervention (because the state is wasteful of resources and limits individual freedoms).
- The importance of league tables which assess the success levels of schools.
- Compulsory education so that minimum standards have been achieved.
- Loans replace universal grants for the most promising students.
- More provision for gifted children.
- The encouragement of certain schools to develop specialisms (such as music, languages, technology or science; some financed in part by private capital).
- The breaking of the power of local education authorities. These were traditionally autonomous and able to organise their own preferred system of education. An alternative structure gives more power to market forces, politicians (hence a national curriculum), individual heads and their governing bodies.

LABOUR IDEOLOGY

This has, since the party was founded in 1906, stood in opposition to that of conservatism. It grew out of the ideas of early socialists; consequently, supporters interpret the nature and causes of social problems and provide alternative ideas about the best organisation of the educational structure. Inevitably, in power, policies do not necessarily reflect the most deeply held values, since once established, structures and systems are difficult to overthrow. Whilst they may ideologically oppose private education, the schools are so entrenched that it would require many years in power and a cultural shift in wider society to push such policies through.

The principal ideals were set out in 1918:

> *to secure for producers by hand or by brain the full fruits of their industry, and the most equitable distribution thereof that may be possible on the basis of the common ownership of the means of production and the best obtainable system of popular administration and control of each industry and service.*

Whilst various amendments have been made to these aims the implications remain that the ideology of Labour is different to that of conservatism. The beliefs imply the promotion of policies to achieve:

- Equality of opportunity. This has been described by **Crossland** (1981) as 'the strongest ethical inspiration of virtually every socialist doctrine and still remains the most characteristic feature of socialist thought.' **Tawney** (1931) said 'The resentment against social inequality is the characteristic of class antagonism'. It would not mean everyone gaining the same qualifications or the same income.
- Freedom, which rests on equality and provides liberty to control one's own life.
- Fellowship; fraternity; community; democracy and humanitarianism.

It is believed by the proponents of this ideology that in a state in which these ideals were pursued, there would be maximum social unity, efficiency, justice and opportunities for self-realization. They would defeat the imbalances caused by the capitalist economic system and all the consequent growth of social ills, waste of ability and inhumanity.

Crossland said 'every child has a natural right as a citizen to life, liberty and the pursuit of happiness and also to a position in the social scale to which his natural talents entitle him'. Inequality in education frustrates this natural right.

Chitty made the point that there was a genuine attempt by the Labour governments of the 1960s and 70s 'to ameliorate the harsh correlation between educational opportunity and the class-and-occupational structure of the nation'. This, however, was frustrated by the incoming Conservative government which was 'more determined than ever to create a divided system, particularly at the secondary level, which discriminated against the vast majority of working class children'.

The consequences for education

This ideology promotes values which includes:

- Support for the comprehensive school (first introduced in 1946, but expanded greatly after 1964).
- Opposition to streaming, setting and specialization.
- More equitable distribution of educational resources between classes: **Chitty** notes that before it was abolished in 1990 by the Conservative government 'the Inner London Education Authority operated its own unique system of banding ... ensuring that each school received its fair share of above and below average pupils.'
- Opposition to private schooling.
- Positive discrimination to assist the students who need more help.
- More help for educationally deprived areas or zones.
- Expansion of both nursery and higher education.

SHOULD SCHOOLS PLACE GREATER EMPHASIS ON TRAINING FOR SPECIFIC OCCUPATIONS?

Activity

It was reported on 21 July 1997 that Baroness Thatcher wants to establish a Professorship of Economic Free Enterprise at Cambridge University. Her Foundation would provide £1.9 million to set it up. The aim would be to promote her ideological economic views. In their comment, the Guardian editorial proclaimed, 'Beware ideologues, even bearing gifts. What would have happened in the past,' they ask, 'if a left wing business man or woman had offered a similar amount to set up a Professorship of Socialist Achievement?'

Answer the following questions?

1. What is meant by ideologues?
2. What view might a functionalist take of the gift?
3. What view might a Marxist express?

NEW LABOUR IDEOLOGY

New Labour (1997) represented a compromise between the traditional and the socialist conceptions of the values of freedom, individualism and inequality. The aims included:

- Greater regional justice in the distribution of resources for children and schools (hence the introduction of Education Action Zones)
- Provision of better opportunities for adult education and early leavers
- Limiting the opportunities children have of moving into private education (abolition of assisted places)
- More emphasis on the principle of equality
- Limiting the opportunities for selection
- Ending opportunities for schools to take grant-maintained status and opt out of the state system.

Study point

In 1999 the Prime Minister said comprehensive schools should make the most of their facilities, increase out-of-hours facilities by entering business and community partnerships; seek excellence and diversity; emphasise modern languages and prioritise numeracy and literacy strategies. What are your views?

EDUCATION: A LIBERAL IDEOLOGY

The liberal educational ideology is not a sociological perspective and promotes themes and ideas of democracy, progress, meritocracy and modernity. The belief is in maximising individual liberty and choice. This liberal approach has been significant in many ways:

- The use of teaching methods employed in Britain known as 'child centred' approaches.
- Special programmes such as Operation Headstart in the USA and EPAs (Educational Priority Areas) and Educational Action Zones, all designed to assist individuals in schools in areas with greatest needs.
- Promoting the concept of a meritocracy and the attack on privileged access to institutions of learning and the expansion of qualifications and examinations to suit all needs.

NEW RIGHT IDEOLOGY

The New Right consists of politicians, intellectuals, academics and others whose aim is to develop and present new right wing policies and explanations for social and economic change.

They argue that a wider, more innovative range of schooling is required. It claims that the public sector is too rigid, with the inhibiting demands of the national curriculum and those of standardization. This limits individual freedom to learn in different ways. They call for more entrepreneurial individualism.

As the economy changes from the traditional industrial base to one of much greater self employment, with more people based in offices or working from home through new technological innovations, this will have an impact on the nature of education. A more self-reliant workforce would develop new cultural attitudes, so that they would encourage their children to buy into a range of educational and welfare packages to suit their changing skills and needs. The future economy will require people to be flexible so that value can be gained from new ideas. The emphasis will be on producing knowledge entrepreneurs; traditional routes through well established universities will be as valuable as any other which produces successful results, the old boy network and contacts, through self-publicity or other talents.

On this view there is justification for the beliefs that:

- Education can be used to promote and facilitate necessary changes in economic life by developing the most valuable skills that will be required in the future.
- The increase in choice, options, competition and standards are the key tools to achieve the desired ends.

- Inefficient, costly state bureaucracies (including colleges, universities and schools) can be attacked.
- Colleges must increase numbers attending or lose funding. Those with poor success rates will close.
- School league tables to be published to compare and contrast results.

Points of evaluation
The demands for educational reforms has led to some contradictions in the arguments of New Right analysts.

- Some advocate the return to traditional approaches: Latin and Greek, English grammar and other features of the traditional curriculum.
- Others attack the standardization and uniformity of the curriculum and press for more business studies, technology and computer based subjects.
- Some favour league tables; others oppose the use of tests and argue for diversity.
- Good marketing became a crucial feature of education in the 1990s. Whilst the aim was to provide parents with greater choice, in reality the schools choose and can find ways of rejecting pupils they do not think will enhance their success rates.

SUMMARY

An ideology is a form of organised belief system which:

- Is concerned with the role of ideas.
- Shapes social behaviour and attitudes.
- Provides ways of explaining the world, serving as a source of social cement, holding groups together.
- Helps power-holders retain their authority, as defenders of the ideological beliefs.
- Forms the basis of every political party. Ideological beliefs vary between each party and so shape the kinds of policies they put in place. They are especially relevant to their views about appropriate educational structures.

STUDY GUIDE

Exam Tips

1 Every question is designed to test specific sociological skills. You may be required to interpret data; present your knowledge of evidence and facts; assess evidence, or evaluate it.

2 Be fully aware of the marking schemes. Short questions frequently aim to test your ability to interpret or extract data.

3 Other questions test skills which require detailed recall of facts from research. Be sure to include details from studies.

Revision Tips

1 Practise answering short questions which offer a few marks for understanding information. If the question asks for three reasons, be sure to offer three different ones.

2 Practise reading tables of statistics or other data. Be sure you can understand them. Make the information relevant by telling someone the facts.

3 Ensure that you can use the concepts and terminology correctly. Keep a notebook in which definitions are listed. Use them in your answers as appropriate, rather than a 'lay persons' language.

Practice Questions

1 Account for the changing structure of the educational system in England and Wales since 1944.

2 Belief in Comprehensive education is as ideological as that of a belief in the value of independent schools. Discuss.

3 Assess the view that schools are both agencies of social conrol and social change.

3

A CONSENSUS THEORY OF EDUCATION

Introduction

THIS CHAPTER EXAMINES the views of the consensus functionalist perspective in understanding the role of education and training. It is this view which links the school to the wider economy in positive ways. The school has always prepared people for their occupational roles by socialising them into acceptable patterns of behaviour and allocating different levels of qualification and training. It also promotes cultural reproduction, introducing them to the wider culture of their society. In Britain, educational research following this perspective has examined many important areas and from which subsequent policy changes have originated, especially those relating to new curriculum and vocational qualifications and opportunities.

KEY AUTHORS	KEY CONCEPTS	KEY ISSUES
Hobbes	Social order	What is the source of social order
Durkheim	Socialisation	Society takes precedence over the individual
Talcott Parsons	Functionalism	What are the functions of the educational system in a modern society?
	Dysfunction	The unintended consequences of rules need to be explained
	Role allocation	Schools provide roles and pass
	Cultural reproduction	on cultural values

Table 3: *Key Authors, Concepts and Issues in this Chapter*

Ricks and Pryke	Overt curriculum Hidden curriculum	Both the official and unofficial curriculum play a role in shaping self-image and attitudes

There are four main categories of sociological theory.

(i)   Macro sociology
  • Functionalist/consensus theory
  • Marxism and neo Marxism: conflict theory (see Chapter 4)
(ii) Micro sociology (see Chapter 5)
  • Phenomenology
  • Symbolic interactionism
  • Ethnomethodology
(iii) Attempts to unite (see Chapter 6)
  • Structuration theory
(iv) Rejection of traditional models
  • Postmodernism theory.

These categories are often described as 'sociological perspectives'. They provide ways of interpreting the social world and the patterns of behaviour which are observed. They are derived from sets of principles or philosophies about the ways in which the social world is organised. The assumption of functionalism is that societal order is the key factor for sociological explanation and analysis.

FUNCTIONALISM AND EDUCATION, A CLASSICAL PERSPECTIVE

Sociologists who undertake research using the model which Durkheim established, see society as being made up of interrelated parts, like cogs in a machine. Each has special functions to perform for the maintenance of the whole system. There are others involved in advising or directing aspects of school life who work within a closely related liberal functionalist perspective because it is the most practical way in which to do their job. For example, they may wish to know why a school is failing, why some teachers are less efficient than others, or why there is a skills shortage in certain areas. If they produce their reports and statements in terms of the structure of the school and its relationship to local or wider national issues and question the effectiveness of teaching methods or recommend new vocational courses, they are approaching the issues as functionalists.

Hobbes, a philosopher writing in the middle of the seventeenth century, raised the problem of explaining how societies established a sense of order and harmony, asking how it was achieved and why it was essential. Why is there not a constant war of everyone against everyone?

Durkheim, writing at the end of the nineteenth century, answered the question by stating that people need to be socialised into the central values of the society to see that order is essential for the good society. In this way, he said that society took precedence over the individual. He noted that there are agencies and organisational structures which control the behaviour of individuals. The educational system was one such key institution.

Parsons (1968) produced important ideas about functionalist perspectives in relation to education in the mid twentieth century. He described how social institutions function to ensure that the principles of a common morality are established to achieve order. Rules and sanctions are needed to control deviance. He said that people act and react with each other everyday in situations controlled by norms. These pattern behaviour and also provide a sense of order and stability within the system or institution.

THE FUNCTIONS OF THE EDUCATIONAL SYSTEM

TO SOCIALISE PUPILS

Durkheim said that the most important concepts in an analysis of society, its rules of order and explanations for disorder are those of function and structure. The educational system defines and promotes the values of a society. Each generation can be taught what is important knowledge and what is considered to be good and bad ways of behaving. In this way, schooling is seen as a process by which new members of society are socialised into becoming good and valuable citizens.

Socialisation

In every society there is a need for people to behave in socially acceptable ways, to adopt the values of the society and operate with moral codes which embody the main belief systems of the society. These are part of the social culture. Without shared values people may become disruptive and social disharmony could result. The socialisation process may require the imposition (or threat) of sanctions to ensure that people obey rules. It also occurs as people interact together and observe the social rules which operate. The family is one agency of socialisation and social control, but the educational system is another. In school, or other educational institutions, children and young people can be formally trained, through the curriculum, and in less formal situations. They come to learn what is and what is not acceptable behaviour, what kind of people they are and what is expected of them. In this way, values, beliefs and perceptions are shaped by the socialisation processes to which they are subjected.

TO ALLOCATE PEOPLE TO SUITABLE WORK ROLES

For functionalists, one of the functions of the educational system is that of selection according to talents. The most able are directed to those areas of work for which their abilities are most required and vice versa. The examination system becomes a crucial tool for allocating people to roles in accordance with skill levels measured objectively. Such qualifications are said to reflect an individual's motivation levels and their potential. Failure is functional because those with fewest qualifications are likely to be allotted the least favourable jobs.

Study point
Having too many well-qualified people could be dysfunctional for society. Explain this.

TO PROMOTE EFFECTIVE MEANS OF TRANSFERRING KNOWLEDGE

Functionalists emphasise the need for schools to encourage skills in those areas of work and study which are of special value to society. Teachers must:

- Encourage group values before individualistic ones. The long-term goals of society and its survival must take precedence over sectional ones.
- Ensure that pupils display all their talents most effectively so they attain their potential and find a place in the economic system as good employees.

TO ASSIST IN THE TRAINING OF FUTURE WORKERS

In the 1990s it became clear that the steady improvement in the economic growth of British society involved further changes in the structure of the educational system still further. It became necessary to introduce means of monitoring the standards in schools. There was agreement about the need for investment in training to ensure that future workers would be equipped with the skills needed for the economy of the twenty-first century. Policies were introduced to encourage vocational courses and enable more pupils to attain relevant qualifications.

TO ENSURE CULTURAL REPRODUCTION BETWEEN GENERATIONS

The overt curriculum

From a functionalist perspective, the curriculum must promote a skilled, well educated workforce in order to produce an effective, growing economy. Inevitably, such ideals are affected from time to time by economic recessions, crises which affect the intended aims and more significantly changing political values about the organisation of the educational system. The 1988 Education Act introduced the national curriculum, with core subjects in which pupils were to be tested (SATs) and other foundation subjects, with attainment targets in each. Amendments were made following debates and recommendations from teachers, parents and administrators.

This national curriculum fits well into a functionalist perspective because it aims 'to promote the spiritual, moral, cultural, mental and physical development of pupils at school and of society.' Furthermore, its stated aim was to prepare pupils for 'the opportunities, responsibility and experiences of adult life.' Whilst there may be problems which arise in delivering the various aspects of the national curriculum, its aims and objectives would be valued by those who argue that schools must clearly state what pupils must know and be expected to achieve in different age groups, to enable them to take an effective and constructive role in the future well-being of their society.

Study point
Why might some people argue that sociology should not be on the curriculum?

The hidden curriculum

Ricks and Pryke (1973) show how the classroom is a place in which learning goes on outside the official curriculum. Pupils pick up signals and communications from teachers about their expectations. For example, children placed in an A stream are often more highly considered than those in the C stream. There may be comments about a girl's appearance and a boy's achievement; different standards of behaviour may be tolerated; boys move furniture, girls tidy up. They interpret statements which enable them to see that some children within the same classroom are perceived in different ways by teachers. Boys may be asked more demanding questions in maths and science lessons; they learn how to impress particular teachers or how to avoid unnecessary work. Pupils develop self-images of their own worth and skills within the school (which may seriously underestimate their talents, but affect their performances).

From a functionalist perspective, the pupil will gain additional advantage by becoming socialised into the particularly valuable ideas of the importance of punctuality, the benefits of hard work and honesty. Positive ideas about the importance of effort, compromise, cooperation, goals of success and moral codes to guide behaviour, will assist them later when they face selection and allocation in the workplace. Those who absorb the more negative aspects of the hidden curriculum (negative labels, the marginalisation of those in lower-class or lower-streamed groups) will lose status, face sanctions and have to accept an inferior role in wider society.

Some commentators have suggested that levels of delinquency vary between schools and suggest that the school itself can have an influence on this behaviour. Where deviancy has become a powerful subculture within the school, these values may also be culturally reproduced. For the functionalist, such patterns would be described as dysfunctional, and would lead the management of the school to locate the areas of danger and remedy them.

CONCLUSIONS

The functionalist perspective lays emphasis on three contributions made by education to the stability of society; in particular, the ways in which it:

(i)   Promotes social solidarity by transmitting the important norms and values of a society from one generation to the next.

(ii) Promotes cooperation through the learning of social rules of behaviour. These are backed up by sanctions. People are socialised effectively.

(iii) Develops all those special skills needed in society, especially where there is division of labour. People are able to locate their most appropriate role in society as adults as a result of their experiences in school.

Points of Evaluation

Whilst there are some points of criticism that can be levelled at the approach, there are some features which make it an appealing way of looking at education. The educational system does seem to have a series of useful functions:

- It provides the necessary knowledge for modern living.
- It is a means of allocating people to the most suitable social and economic roles.
- It is a source of important norms and social values. After a revolution, the new rulers invariably seize control of the media and the educational system to promote their new ideologies.
- It is a source of a person's self-image; generally, most people come to accept outcomes of their education as indications of their ability levels. They believe that if they have not done well, it was because they have not tried hard enough. In this way the educational system is assumed to be fair and largely meritocratic and that people get from it as much as they are prepared to put into it in effort.
- Functionalist analysis provides evidence of a connection between class background and educational attainment, related to cultural differences.
- Functionalists present evidence for the socialisation processes both through formal methods (training and sanctions) and informal ones (peers, hidden curriculum).

The points of criticism

These tend to be more theoretical, arising from the philosophical ideas on which the perspective of functionalism is based. For example:

1   The functionalist analysis has a conservative basis. Its proponents are suspicious of any radical developments within the educational system. Some subjects are criticised as failing to provide a functionally useful purpose. (The Chief Inspector expressed opposition to the teaching of Media Studies; other subjects (such as Sociology) may be seen as potentially subversive. Functionalism places more emphasis on the production of like-minded people in broad agreement about how to achieve a stable society. This would account for why the teaching of religious values would be highly valued.

2   In view of the widely varying value systems to which people subscribe (cohabitation rather than marriage; non-religious attitudes; competitive beliefs as opposed to co-operative ones) it is not certain that schools do promote shared moral codes.

3   Whilst people may assume that the educational system operates in a fair and just way, rewarding the best and limiting the rewards of those who are less able, the perspective plays down the impact of major social inequalities as explanations for failure. David Blunkett (Secretary of State for Education, in 2000) stated that poverty was no excuse for failing in school. He implies that a well organised educational establishment should override economic disadvantage. This issue is of much greater concern to the conflict theorists.

SUMMARY

The principles of functionalism are based on conservative, consensual values. Marxist perspectives are based on ideas of conflict and oppositional values. Interactional perspectives arise from interpretive influences on behaviour in processes of everyday life. More recent perspectives have endeavoured either to find ways of uniting the classical approaches to develop a more contemporary analysis, or of dismissing them and reasserting more relativist interpretations. The structural functional approach is designed to understand the processes which help to maintain the order and the consensus (agreements about how to behave) in the system. It lays great emphasis on the power of the school to socialise, allocate roles and provide important vocational training, for the long term stability of society itself.

Group Work

1 Adopt the perspective of a functionalist and through group discussion: Draw up a list of the overt curriculum that operates in the institution in which you are studying. Include the areas which are non-examinable. Identify key aspects of the hidden curriculum. Look at the positive and the negative features. Write a short report which would include constructive recommendations for the management of the institution making them aware of the strengths and weaknesses identified.

Coursework Suggestions

1 Undertake a study to ascertain the range of norms which influence behaviour in a classroom. How are they identifiable? How do they get observed and learned? What happens if members of the group disregard them? What kind of sanctions come into play? Consider ways of identifying the norms: can both interviews and observational methods be used appropriately?

Exam Hints

1 If you have done the requisite work you should pass the exam. Be confident.
2 A mild degree of stress is useful; high levels of anxiety are disruptive.
3 Don't leave the exam before the end of the allotted time. Check answers.

Revision Tips

1 Check the syllabus to ensure you are aware of all the areas to be covered.
2 Analyse the questions below and check that you understand what each one is asking. Answer one in about 800 words.

Practice Questions

1 Assess functionalist approaches to an understanding of the significance of socialisation, vocational curriculum and cultural reproduction.
2 Examine the strengths and weaknesses of the view that a well-educated and skilled work-force will promote greater social solidarity.
3 Discuss the argument that both success and failure in the educational system are functional.

4

CONFLICT PERSPECTIVES IN EDUCATION

Introduction

THIS CHAPTER EXAMINES the arguments of conflict theorists whose views oppose those of functionalists. Conflict explanations examine similar issues, but start from the problems arising from the structure of capitalist society, in which different groups share opposing interests. The attainments of children vary between these groups, some benefiting more than others from the same educational system. It is the economic infrastructure which affects lifestyle and life chances. The capitalist system has certain requirements for its maintenance, which the educational system provides. These include the values of competition, status and hierarchies of power. It allocates people into particular occupational roles through competitive examinations and other processes by which the able are distinguished from the less able. It does not promote high level skills among the lower working class; this sector is always required as a reserve army of labour to do the least skilled work. This perspective presents a more critical view of education than that of the functionalist analysis.

Table 4: *Key Authors, Concepts and Issues in this Chapter*		
KEY AUTHORS	KEY CONCEPTS	KEY ISSUES
Giddens	Power	Groups compete for power
Marx	Power elites	Those which control the key institution are the most powerful
	Alienation	Tedious work and exploitation produces a sense of misery

Bowles and Gintis	Compliant workers	The educational system can produce conforming workers
Bordieu	Cutural capital	The most successful in the educational system have inherited most cultural capital
Althusser	Ideological state apparatus	The means by which the powerful achieve control over the weak
Sharp and Green	Teacher perception	The child's ability level is assessed by teachers' impressionistic assessments
Willis	Working-class culture	Alienated working-class youth use their cultural values as a source of resistance
Milliband	Conspiracy theory	The educational system can be used to delude the working class
Reeves	New vocationalism	A change to a mass democratic educational participation would assist alienated working-class students
Anyon	Dominant ideology	Even textbooks perpetuate the values of the power elites
Measor	Gender differentiation	The curriculum perpetuates gender inequalities
Head	Hidden curriculum	The means by which pupils gain additional insights into how they are valued

KEY ISSUES

The perspectives derive from Marx and later neo-Marxists, but also includes feminist research and Weberian concerns about the ways that education confers status distinctions which affect the life chances of people. The issues on which such theorists focus, in their explanation of the inequalities affecting educational opportunities, are both inside and outside the school. In wider society there are problems arising from patterns of socialisation; the distribution of power and class alienation. Social inequality is perpetuated and reproduced inside the school through teacher perception of attainments, of gender and ethnicity; also the effects of the curriculum, systems of vocational training and the distribution of qualifications. Its proponents emphasise that the Marxian claim is an optimistic one. People can influence their own creative development, when made aware of the forces which otherwise limit their horizons. Then they will act in their own interests rather than those of another class.

SOCIALISATION

There is no disagreement among conflict and consensus theorists that there are several powerful sources of socialisation in society, which inculcate values leading to an acceptance of the status quo. These occur within the family, through the mass media and via the educational system, all of which function to control pupils and shape attitudes and values of compliance to the needs of society. Those who comply with the demands will achieve success; those who do not will have fewer choices and opportunities. For the functionalists, stability is based on the assimilation of agreed values that benefit the whole of society. For conflict theorists, the processes of socialisation teach values which represent the dominant ideology of the most powerful, those who control the economic system for their own advantage or that of their class.

POWER

Giddens (1989) defines power as 'the capability of actors to secure outcomes' (over others who would have acted differently if the power had not been exercised). In a class-divided society, people unite with those who share a common relation to the processes of production. The conflict theorists examine how the dominant groups are able to legitimise their power and ensure that there are institutions in society which will produce and reproduce the conditions necessary to sustain their control. Power differentials are seen everywhere in society: those in the highest class groups form power elites, and are able to define certain ideas and practices as superior to any alternatives. Conflict theorists argue that these are imposed on others as the proper and acceptable ways of thinking in a class society. The result is:

- Polarisation of the division of labour between the owners of the means of production and those who are employees.
- Exploitation, to which the wage-labourers acquiesce, to ensure that they remain in work.
- An effectively compliant work-force provided by the vocational training systems in schools.
- The continued control of social and economic institutions by wealthy power elites.

ALIENATION

Marx used the concept of alienation to describe the consequences of the exploitation of workers within the capitalist system. The worker is separated from sense of worth. In their discussions of the experiences of education among many working class children, conflict theorists also make use of it, to explain why there is:

- A failure to gain any sense of personal value from schooling.
- A constant sense of misery, unhappiness or futility in work.
- A lack of motivation; the student is alienated from curriculum content and controlled through grades and marks, rather than being integrated in the processes of learning.
- Frequent humiliation for the child; competition can be destructive to confidence but operates under the guise of merit, ranking and evaluation.
- Much greater satisfaction in leisure time.
- A lack of autonomy and control over their own lives. The alien character of school work is shown by the fact that when there is no compulsion or sanction being imposed, it is avoided like the plague.
- Social distinction dividing pupils in every school, because it is a microcosm of wider society.

Study point
How might a functionalist suggest that alienated pupils could be reintegrated into a school?

CULTURAL REPRODUCTION

This has been examined by researchers adopting a critical perspective. For example:

(i) **Bowles and Gintis** (1976) argued that the ways in which the school is organised and the principles on which it operates closely reflect the structure of wider society. In both there is a requirement for the maintenance of:

- A hierarchy of power; with clear divisions between status based on ability.
- A large group who will follow basic rules and instructions (especially at the lowest end of the work spectrum).

- A group who will show dependability, punctuality and independence for positions of management responsibility and show adherence to the norms of hard efficient work.

They showed that the longer students stayed within the educational system, the more likely they were to adopt the norms required for management positions. The school produced and reproduced the values which correlated closely with socio-economic class position. They conclude that the social class background of pupils is of central importance in determining their school attainment and final position in the job market.

(ii) **Bordieu** (1973) explained how schools reflect social inequalities by ensuring that the greatest rewards go to those whose backgrounds provide them with the most **cultural capital**. That is, an appreciation and ability to interpret and use the codes which carry the dominant culture and the important knowledge which is required for school and examination success and which eventually provides economic power.

- Those who have limited amounts of such cultural capital are more likely to become eliminated from the opportunities which exist within the educational system. Either they will opt out at the earliest opportunity or be driven out through academic failures.
- These assets are transferred from generation to generation as children are socialised into the norms and values of family and school life.

(iii) **Althusser** (1972) argued that the educational system serves to mould young people into deferential workers, who will support the existing system, in accordance with the demands and interests of the ruling class. It is an example of an **ideological state apparatus** (others include religion, family and media) designed to achieve control, by mystifying and deluding people. Religion gives them the myths, the customary rules of family life provides the training and socialisation, and education the disciplines backed by sanctions to achieve the required ends. These ideological systems of beliefs:

- Instill in people a comprehensible view of the world and how to behave in it.
- Inhibit social change and mobility since the status quo is seen to be the ideal.

Points of evaluation
The view that working-class children have limited social mobility because they lack cultural capital may have some validity at the lowest end of the social scale. For the majority, especially those from homes in which parents are skilled manual workers, the cultural differences between them and middle-class children is less relevant. The popular television programmes, newspapers and music which carry the shared culture of the majority are as familiar in one as in the other. There is also the danger of assuming that all working-class children are

unable to achieve any academic success, or that all middle-class children are successful in school.

(iv) **Sharp and Green** (1975) noted how even in a progressive primary school, teachers developed strategies to deal with a range of pupils who posed various problems for them. They used these to distinguish between the bright, the normal and the difficult. These reflected class differences in society outside the school, whilst the life chances of the children were being structured at an early stage within it. They recognised that this was not a deliberate matter on the part of the teachers to impose categories of differentiation, but rather it was the outcome of the constraints and demands of the classroom, in which they had to resolve their work problems.

(v) **Paul Willis** (1977) used observational methods to examine the attitudes of a small group of disaffected working class pupils, described as 'the lads'. He showed how these boys were not passive recipients of 'education' in their school. They used their strong working class culture as a means of resistance; their values of aggression, sexism, racism and masculinity provided them with a means to cope with what they saw as a largely pointless attempt to educate them. From a conflict perspective, they seemed to see through the deception which the ruling class had imposed. They knew that the schooling system was unfair in that it differentiated between children from different cultural backgrounds. They knew that they would inevitably end up in mundane jobs. The culture which they duly encountered there embodied the same values that they had expressed negatively in school. This was also used in the workplace as a means of regaining some control over their lives, by finding ways of coping with the tedium of their work. It is ironical that as a result, their patterns of behaviour served to sustain the ideology they knew was oppressing them. In a sense, they contributed to their own exploitation.

Study point
Milliband has said 'the educational system conspires to create the impression not least among its victims, that social disadvantages are really a matter of personal, innate, God-given and insurmountable incapacity.' What does he mean and do you agree?

Points of evaluation

1 There is a danger for writers who adopt a conflict perspective becoming partial in their comments relating to the groups they observe. **Willis**, for example, has been accused of accepting and celebrating the views of the twelve members of the group he studied. It is difficult to generalise from a small sample about working class culture in general.

2   There is the implication that work attitudes are shaped by educational experiences. It is assumed that where these are negative, then day to day work will also be distasteful. Yet for many workers in routine occupations, their work can be valued as an enjoyable experience. It is where their social life is developed. In the same way, many people in professions may find aspects of their work tedious or stressful.

3   Many middle class pupils are equally bored by particular teachers or adopt anti-school cultural styles (for example, to modify school uniforms to suit trends in fashion). The pupils Willis studied were not acting as docile and compliant workers.

4   There is the problem for some conflict theorists of seeing human beings as almost entirely passive and deterministic creatures, who are shaped by the economic system in their unthinking acceptance of the status quo. This image is undermined by the work of Willis who sees the pupils he studied as very active and in control of their destinies.

VOCATIONAL TRAINING

Whereas functionalists argue that schools increasingly provide valuable vocational training for work, conflict theorists, such as **Braverman** and **Willis**, have argued that working-class pupils are deskilled by rapid technological developments. In automated processes they become button pushers and so lose much of the power they once had in heavy industrial plants. By streaming and setting examination students, the weakest (invariably those in the lowest socio-economic groups) have their opportunities depressed.

Reeves (1997) argued for a new vocationalism, which had 'little to do with the divisive policies pursued by previous governments, and everything to do with the economic empowerment of local citizens.' He noted how the existing anachronistic forms of education continued to serve middle class interests; these needed to be displaced in favour of mass democratic educational participation, even if this entailed forging links with the wealth creating mechanisms of society. He said: 'Colleges with large student populations, a third of whom may be unemployed and over three quarters aged over 20, provide a clear challenge to educationalists committed to providing education and training relevant to its local community.'

THE OVERT CURRICULUM

The official curriculum is that which appears as time-tabled subjects containing all that information considered necessary for children in schools and colleges, much of which may be subject to legal requirement. Conflict theorists have raised a number of questions about the values it implies. Reeves says: 'the selection by inclusion or omission of material for the school curriculum undoubtedly results in the representation by teachers and assimilation by students, of a particular set of cultural and political values.'

The great ninteenth century thinkers, Darwin, Marx and Freud are generally ommitted, or handled gingerly and usually with hostility, in the sixth form.

Study point
Reeves asks whether and in what manner, the reader was taught about issues such as republicanism, humanism, atheism, communism, or issues such as the feminist movement, euthanasia, abortion on demand and the gay movement. What is your experience?

Milliband (1991) comments on the influence of ethnocentric approaches to issues and the assumption of consensual values of much material dealt with in the curriculum, and from which the pupils and students themselves are alienated.

Anyon (1977) argues that apart from the teaching styles, the content of the textbooks used presents material which reflects the interests of ruling elite groups. These books both express the ideologies of these dominant groups and help to shape attitudes in support of them.

Measor (1983) suggests that the curriculum and the ways in which the teacher deals with classroom issues arising from it sustain gender differentiation of subject skills.

THE HIDDEN CURRICULUM

From a conflict perspective, the hidden curriculum is not a valuable addition to day-to-day learning, about punctuality, good manners and observing rules of conduct. Rather, it is seen as a means of achieving additional controls over pupils in both formal and informal settings. There are many subtle messages conveyed to pupils which they will assimilate and which will affect their behaviour and responses to the school.

Head (1974) says the hidden curriculum describes the rules which pupils learn in order to survive. It is all the other things learnt in school, to cope with problems, with delay, with teachers, with other pupils and with the demands of school life. They may learn how to feign interest and understanding where both are lacking. In school situations, they learn:

- To internalise self-images based on teacher perception ('non-academic'; 'clever'; 'nuisance').

- Their social status and what kind of job would suit them as a result.
- To accept a hierarchy of power and how to cope with repetitious or tedious work.
- The merits and weaknesses of the reward-and-punishment systems.
- To draw significance from the system of streams and sets for self-image.
- The structure of the staffing; who are the most important and powerful.
- The implications of the ways that responsibilities are distributed between males and females and how to deal effectively with disgruntled staff.

Points of evaluation
The conflict theorists claim:

(i) That the overt curriculum is designed to promote the benefits of a capitalist economic system, and the hidden one is another of the tools by which children are indoctrinated into the values of the ruling class.

Critics respond that:

- Apart from some specially vocational colleges, most pupils do not study subjects which promote success in the marketplace.
- Academic disciplines may also encourage questioning and promote a critical approach (especially true of a subject like sociology).
- Teachers are constrained from encouraging an active, questioning classroom because of the demands of trying to teach 30 or more pupils.
- There is no clear definition of what the hidden curriculum means or what its content is.

(ii) That since educational reforms from 1988 the State has become more concerned to impose controls over teachers and how and what they teach, ensuring that the status quo is maintained.

The outcome has been that some colleges run by management with more radical agendas have suffered and in some cases been closed.

Critics respond that:

- The claims of employers that standards were too low influenced policy in positive ways.
- Postmodernists argue that all work has become more fragmentary and flexible; reskilling occurs and more pupils are receiving necessary training in a variety of skills. Schools must represent pluralism and difference.

SUMMARY

The conflict perspective is based on Marxist principles that capitalism brings differential rewards. Those who do most to sustain the system gain the least. This structure produces different class groups based on their relationship to the production processes. The educational system mirrors this structure, with its graded hierarchy of power and authority. The inequalities result in exploitation and loss of talent. In their critique conflict theorists argue that the formal organisation of education is little more than one to generate myths to delude and control the largely working-class membership. It legitimates inequality; it leads people to assume that educational and occupational success is based on merit and that role and status allocation in adult life are open and fair. These values are promoted through the ideological state apparatuses and sustained by the repressive state apparatuses (the courts, the police and the military). Discontent is controlled and major social inequalities in the distribution of wealth and power are accepted as normal. Educational reforms are not likely to be very effective in changing the way the schools reproduce the social system; they will continue to work in the interests of power elites.

STUDY GUIDE

Revision Tips

1 Regular revision is much more effective than last minute revision.
2 Ensure that you understand the issues you are revising, so that you have a complete picture.
3 Make a list of things to be revised and an appropriate order.

Practice Questions

1 The educational attainment of different social groups is directly related to the amount of cultural capital they possess. The educational system is not a means of social transformation. Discuss.
2 Assess the view that schools legitimate inequality and can never be meritocratic.
3 Outline and assess the Marxist analysis of schooling in modern Britain.

5

INTERPRETATIVE PERSPECTIVES

Introduction

THIS CHAPTER EXAMINES evidence from an interpretative perspective. It is based on the ways in which teachers and pupils interact in social situations, within educational institutions. The perspective places emphasis on the subjective interpretations of actors, that is, the meanings which people take from their interactions as the basis for their subsequent behaviour. People develop their self-image from the ways they are treated by others; they may also modify their behaviour if it is inappropriate and results in problems, or intensify it according to rewards. It is an approach which has been useful (in conjunction with others) for understanding patterns of behaviour based on classroom observations.

Table 5: *Key Authors, Concepts and Issues in this Chapter*		
KEY AUTHORS	KEY CONCEPTS	KEY ISSUES
Mead Blumer	Interactionism	How do people make sense of their experiences?
Goffman Schutz	Social construction of reality Phenomenology	How does role affect behaviour? How do people establish meaning in their lives?
Garfinkel	Ethnomethodology	How can the taken-for granted rules of social life be uncovered?

Willis	Participant oberservation	What are the problems of observation in classrooms?
Becker	Non-participant oberservation	
Rist	Labelling	What is the process of having a label attached to a pupil?
Cicourel and Kitsuse	Teacher perception	How are pupils evaluated by teachers?
Goode and Brophey		
Keddie	Classroom knowledge	
Becker	Ideal student	
Sharma and Meighan	Self-fulfilling prophecy	The significance of gender
Mirza	Negative labels	
Hargreaves	Streaming	The pupil perception
Maizels	Good and bad teachers	
Meighan	Hidden curriculum	
Rex	Racism	The issues of ethnicity
Little	Ethnic minorities	

MICRO PERSPECTIVES

There are several interpretative approaches which share much in common. They tend to be micro perspectives (looking at the small scale areas of social life, in places where people congregate together) and all are critical of the positivist, scientific approaches of the macro sociologists, who utilize questionnaires, interviews and statistical methods. But there are some differences between them. Each has a slightly different underlying theory which informs the methods preferred in gathering and interpreting data. They include ethnomethodology; phenomenology; and symbolic interactionism. However, they can be generally described as 'interpretative', 'action' theories and they have proved an important perspective in research, especially in education.

- They view individuals not as puppets being worked by mysterious forces beyond their control, but as being capable of action and reaction.
- Social order is achieved in the actor's lives by the ways they make sense of events and by the ways in which meaning is negotiated. ('I will behave well in your class if you teach me in an inspirational way').
- What a person thinks is the case (even if it is mistaken) will influence subsequent behaviour.

Study point
A teacher appears to misunderstand a comment, interprets it as rudeness and makes an angry response. The pupil looks shocked. The teacher says 'wipe that smirk off your face'. The relationship further deteriorates. The pupil ends in detention. Explain how this might be an example of a self-fulfilling prophecy.

From this perspective, it would not be sufficient to explain a child's failure to obtain qualifications in terms of a single factor, such as class background ('he comes from that estate, what can you expect?') The aim would be to see how the child was perceived by teachers and how the child interpreted his or her experiences in school. The emphasis is on what happens in day to day life, rather than on grand theories involving the wider structure of society.

Mead (1934) saw that the significant fact of human interaction was the importance of symbols, which are encoded in the language used between people. The use of terms implies meaning and action. For example, symbolic terms such as 'teacher', 'pupil', and 'classroom' classify the world and enable people to make sense of it. In schools pupils, students and teachers are constantly in processes of interaction which give rise to all kinds of outcomes. School subcultures emerge, some promote educational success, others seek to oppose and reject it.

Blumer (1969) said that the task of the interactionist is to reveal the processes through which people construct their actions. The aim of this analysis is to understand and make clear the outcomes of such interactions.

Goffman (1959) describes social life as a theatrical performance, which makes use of props, sets and roles. The headmaster wears a suit and tie and looks appropriately 'headmasterly'; he has a special office, and ensures that rules and regulations are applied and enforced. The pupil plays a subordinate role; showing deference and responding to instructions. He makes the point that 'when an individual appears before others he will have many motives for trying to control the impression they receive of the situation.' In other words, role playing is a feature of everyone's lives.

PHENOMENOLOGY

Phenomenologists do not think it is possible to find the causes of human behaviour merely by understanding the meanings they have imposed on situations. They claim that no hard factual data can be obtained about social life; statistics are weak instruments which are subject to many major criticisms. The only thing to be done is to show how people come to be defined as 'educationally weak' or 'school nuisance' by examining the ways that teachers make their definitions and the ways that pupils develop meanings from which labels are fixed.

Schutz (1967) said that people build up shared meanings of the world. They send their children to school, knowing that it is organised to provide them with appropriate knowledge. The headteacher assumes that parents will comply with requests that children be punctual and that the children attending will behave in appropriate ways. Such knowledge becomes part of the common sense understanding of the world. It is the way that order is achieved, in what is in reality a fluid and uncertain world.

METHODOLOGIES

Frequently, the situation in which the action being observed takes place does not lend itself to any technique other than observation. A football crowd cannot be constrained to complete questionnaires whilst a match is in progress, nor can children enjoying their playtime, or the bully causing problems, or the busy teacher dealing with a noisy classroom. However, where feasible, many researchers may make use of many procedures. Observations may be followed by questionnaires or interviews following the events, perhaps in the staffroom later or in the child's home, or in a youth club in the evening, from which additional data can be added.

Willis (1977) made use of participant observation because he says it was done 'in the natural situations of the actors'. Also, it enabled him to share experiences with those he observed and see the world more clearly through their eyes. He also made use of his knowledge of the social background of the young men he observed.

Becker (1974) has described the difficulties of observing as a non-participant in classrooms:

> *it is first and foremost a matter of it all being so familiar that it becomes almost impossible to single out events that occur in the classroom as things that have occurred, even when they happen in front of you … it takes a tremendous effort of will and imagination to stop seeing only things that are conventionally 'there' to be seen.*

THE VALUE OF THE PERSPECTIVE

The approach has been valuable because it has provided new insights into many previously neglected aspects of behaviour. These include:

(i)   How labels are attached in the processes of teacher–pupil interaction
(ii) Teacher–pupil perceptions and their effects, with regard to success and failure

(iii) How self-fulfilling prophecies occur
(iv) The significance of gender and ethnicity.

LABELLING THEORIES

Interpretative sociologists have studied the processes by which labels become attached to pupils and students; how some are seen as bright, others as deviant, others as potential troublemakers and so on. Labelling theories suggest that once someone has been defined or labelled in a certain way, then they will be perceived and treated in accordance with the label. Interpretative perspectives enable researchers to view the actors in context to see.

Cicourel and Kitsuse (1963) showed how students were evaluated by teachers and school counsellors in terms of their appearances, their manners and observed patterns of behaviour, although they claimed to be using objective measures, such as IQ and grade results. The process begins when there is initial speculation based on characteristics which the teachers see as valuable. Re-assessments may be made or early assumptions confirmed once the pupil becomes better known to the teacher. There is eventually a fairly stable image established, once reports come to be written and work and attitudes evaluated. Once these labels are firmly attached, for those with more negative assessments, they may be hard to change.

Rist (1977) notes that 'the crux of the labelling perspective lies not in whether one's norm violating behaviour is known, but whether others decide to do something about it.'

Becker made the point that deviance is 'a consequence of the application by others of rules and sanctions to an offender. The deviant is the one to whom the label has been successfully applied.' This application is a complicated process, but where it is successful, the individual can be blighted in their subsequent educational career. Schools which produce high levels of deviants may well be those with the strictest rules, since breaking one sets off the labelling process. This is sometimes referred to as the 'amplification of deviance'.

- The school has strict rules
- Many children break them
- A few break them more frequently
- They also break them out of school (smoking; acts of vandalism)
- They are punished for these in school
- The offenders become more set in their ways and offend more frequently
- They may band together and are increasingly identified as 'the problem' pupils
- They are perceived in more negative ways
- The vicious circle spirals with dangerous consequences for the deviants.

Those schools with fewest rules to break and with more relaxed policies regarding behaviour which is not treated so aggressively, may well have fewest problem children.

Teacher–pupil perceptions

Keddie (1971) criticised the fact that the explanations for educational failure are frequently given in terms of pupils' ethnic and social class backgrounds. She examines the defining procedures occurring within the school itself. She used observational techniques to show how teachers evaluated pupils and established their presumed levels of competence. She found they made use of their knowledge of them in the assessments they made. Children were perceived to be the most able when they had readily absorbed information presented to them. Those who offered less relevant knowledge were seen to be 'less able'. She concluded that the failure of high ability pupils to question what they were taught contributed to their levels of educational achievement and that classroom evaluation of pupils was socially constructed in the processes of interaction.

Goode and Brophey (1973) also showed how teachers behaved differently with the students they assumed were high achievers than they did with those they perceived as less able; which is one of the main reasons for the criticisms levelled at streaming.

Pupil perceptions

Interactionists have also examined the ways that pupils interpret their experiences of the school.

Hargreaves (1967) looked at the ways they responded to the system of streaming, and developed self-images.

Maizels (1970) showed that pupils had clear views about the differences between 'good' and 'bad' teachers, and responded accordingly.

Meighan (1979) showed that pupils are able to recognise aspects of the hidden curriculum, some of the labelling processes and record their feelings of alienation that resulted.

Self-fulfilling prophecies

A self-fulfilling prophecy classically develops from an initial false diagnosis of a person's abilities or personality type. This may be based on their appearance, their gender, knowledge of their home or ethnic background or the way they respond in a classroom. It starts with an assumption; evidence is obtained which appears to support it (counter evidence is ignored), expectations are further developed and produce the expected outcomes.

Becker showed that teachers frequently made their evaluations of pupils and students in terms of how close they approximated to their concept of 'an ideal student'. That is, one who completed good work, in a tidy way, was punctual and conscientious.

WHAT ARE THE ADVANTAGES AND DISADVANTAGES OF CO-EDUCATIONAL SCHOOLS?

Gender and ethnicity

Some teachers may work with the belief that there are innate gender differences in skill levels in different subject areas. For example, they may believe that it is a scientific fact that girls do less well in maths and science because they have weaker spatial abilities than boys. This assumption may lead them to treat girls in the classroom differently.

Sharma and Meighan (1980) showed that girls who were matched on equivalent experience with boys did not lack spatial ability and did equally well in mathematics. What they showed was that girls lacked crucial experiences in developing spatial ability thinking, which meant they were not as likely to perform as well. This became misdiagnosed as a lack of innate biological ability. The girls themselves may lose confidence in abilities they had at 11 and duly learn to fail in mathematics and science in comparison with boys. The way that teachers then perceive gender differences and act on their impressions may result in levels of underachievement among those so treated.

Rex and Tomlinson (1979) pointed out that biology has contributed nothing to the study of race; the definition applied to someone as black or white, English or Welsh is a social description. Interactionists have analysed how racism manifests itself in the responses which teachers make to children in their classrooms, based on assumptions and interpretations.

Meighan has said they may be victims of hidden bias in their well-intentioned work. Researchers have noted the ways in which teachers can be influenced by language problems, a pupil's own self-perception of inferiority, scores on IQ and other tests of attainment and cultural variations (including dress, religious values and home environment).

Little (1975) concluded that: 'Just as the educational system has failed to meet the needs of the child from a working class background, so now, to an even greater extent, it is failing to meet the needs of the child from a different cultural background.' Interactionists have identified some of the causes and consequences of the problems facing ethnic minority children in the processes of observational research.

Points of evaluation
Whilst the interpretative perspective can produce important insights to explain pupil performance, the approach is open to points of criticism.

(i)   The methodology is based on types of observation and interpretation which cannot be tested scientifically.

(ii) There are issues of ethics, which question whether people should be studied covertly.

(iii) There is an implication that negative labelling always produces negative attitudes.

    Mirza (1997) found that black girls worked hard to overcome the potentially damaging negative labels which they knew may be attached to people like themselves.

(iv) There is often a lack of reference to wider society. What the interpretative sociologist sees in the classroom may be a reflection of what can be seen by other researchers outside the school.

(v)   Teachers may object that they are criticised as being biased and prejudiced as controllers of the labelling processes. They are frequently working under pressures and constraints. In fact the processes of labelling and stereotyping are common to everyone in every walk of life. It is one of the methods used to make sense of complicated data quickly.

Study point
Consider whether you have used stereotypes of labelling in the course of the last few days. What were the circumstances?

SUMMARY

The interpretative approaches place useful emphasis on the ways that people derive meanings from their day-to-day interactions and behave in accordance with their assumptions. Instead of suggesting that poor behaviour in school results from poor socialisation, defective home background and subcultural values associated with a particular social class, the interpretative sociologists look at the ways the child interacts with teachers in a classroom and how the teacher makes assessments of behaviour and how labels become attached. Such research has revealed important insights relating to the way children become deviant or less successful in school than their peers. It may also have helped undermine traditional beliefs about the innate differences between boys and girls and the abilities of children of different ethnic backgrounds.

STUDY GUIDE

Group Work

1 Do members of the group have examples and incidents of the labelling process as it has been applied to them or their friends? Are there examples of it applying in both positive and negative ways? Did any try to counter the labels (even those who were perceived as 'very clever')? With what success? Are there any examples of self-fulfilling prophecies? What recommendations can be put forward to make teachers and others more aware of the issues and problems?

2 Consider the range of norms which exist within a classroom or within a school or college, which control patterns of behaviour (in positive and negative ways). How are they passed on through interaction? How might they occur on the school bus? How might they be studied so they are revealed to participants who are unaware of their power over behaviour. Consider norms relating to homework; ways of slowing the pace of a lesson; completing minimal amounts of work; maximising free time; dress codes; language codes; topics of conversation.

Coursework Suggestions

1 Establish the existence, power and influence of pro- and anti-school subcultures through observational techniques.

2 **Gorbutt** (*The New Sociology of Education*) has said that 'we cannot merely describe a school assembly as a consensual ritual which binds staff and pupils together. This indeed may be the stated intention of the headmaster but the interpretation put upon the event by others, even though they may outwardly conform, cannot be assumed.' Undertake a study to examine the various meanings which a school assembly has for staff and pupils.

Exam Tips

1 Avoid post-mortems. They can be depressing.
2 Try to enjoy an examination; you can do so if you are master of your material.
3 Ensure that you are familiar with all the requirements of the examination syllabus.

Revision Tips

1 Use your responsibilities for self-learning seriously.
2 Study in the same place every day and develop a routine of work.
3 Set targets for revision which can be achieved and provide yourself with a reward when you have done so.

Practice Questions

1 Differences in childrens' attitudes towards education and their attainments are socially constructed in the classroom. Discuss.
2 The methodology used to obtain information about teacher expectations and pupil perceptions through classroom observations is open to criticism. Discuss.
3 Teachers perceive some students and pupils as lacking motivation, interest and intelligence. Explain and assess the contribution that interpretative sociology has given to our understanding of success and failure within the school system.

6

CONTEMPORARY THEORIES

Introduction

IN THIS CHAPTER, there is an examination of recent developments in the sociology of education. In sociology in general, there has been the emergence of perspectives and theories which endeavour to overcome the divisions which have characterised sociological research from the 1960s. The emphasis is on developing the pluralistic nature of sociological research which make use of several methods. The idea that they are exclusive and that researchers only use either scientific measures or subjective interpretation is challenged and fresh debates have emerged.

Table 6: *Key Authors, Concepts and Issues in this Chapter*		
KEY AUTHORS	KEY CONCEPTS	KEY ISSUES
Hulme	Critical social research	There is a need for a re-evaluation of methodological approaches
Willis		The value of a combination of research methods
Davies	Post-structuralism	What is seen at surface level is the only subject of study
Usher and Edwards	Postmodernism	Theories which claim insights into absolute truths are misguided
Layder	Realism	A more realistic approach
Gellner	Hysteria of subjectivity	The postmodern position is unable to provide any

Giddens	Structuration	worthwhile insights There is a relationship between structure and action
Habermas	Neo-critical theory	Opposes the neo-conservative implications of postmodernism
Gillborn	Stereotypes	How does the issue of ethnicity affect teacher perceptions?
Herrnstein and Murray Marsland	IQ Bias against business	What is the relevance of IQ? Examples of New Right concern

CRITICAL SOCIAL RESEARCH

The aim is to achieve understanding by examining how processes of interaction and social structures (like schools) produce meanings for people on which to base their behaviour. The researcher adopting this approach in relation to educational performance would examine many related factors; for example, the history of teacher training and its changing methods; the ways the teacher arrives at attitudes and beliefs about pupils in the classroom; the significance of staffroom values; the staff relations with and knowledge of youth cultures and peer group norms; also, ideas about the rights of the child, in the past and in the present. Wide ranging social and economic factors would also be relevant, such as changing employment prospects; the significance of government policies and relevant legal issues; the effects of social class values and the trends in the media in relation to education. The approach is an archaeological one and involves searching both above and below the surface appearances to achieve a new appreciation of the events studied.

Hulme (1999) makes the point that 'critical analysis recognizes that social science is context bound by economic, political and social conflict' and that the outcome has been 'a re-evaluation of methodological approaches.' In her claim for a resistance to the domination of one perspective over another, she emphasises the fact that much sociological research has always been motivated by pragmatic considerations. The work of **Willis** combines interactionist approaches with those of Marxist conflict analysis. He shows how disaffected working-class pupils were able to act on their environmental experiences and their resistance in school to middle-class values shows they are not merely pawns in a large economic conspiracy, but actors who shape their own destinies. Qualifications and academic successes are valueless in their lives. Ironically, they freely enter into a world of inequality. **Hulme** concludes that quantitative and qualitative research approaches can be fruitfully combined in an integrated research strategy.

NEO-CRITICAL THEORY

Habermas (1976) was influenced by both Marx and Weber. He advocates the value of action theory to see how people have goals they wish to achieve, and how they can negotiate through language to achieve agreements in relationships. He presents an optimistic view of future social developments, in which thoughtful policies and improved awareness on the part of teachers, parents and others involved in the educational processes, could produce a better society. He notes the hazards of capitalism in which power elites control knowledge; the value of reason and the power of language. Societies evolve and move from their traditional systems as constructive processes of rationalisation occur through communication and interaction. People can reflect on their behaviour and become educated in what is socially acceptable and valuable. If effective communication between people is the central prerequisite for cooperative action, and for the ultimate goal of personal emancipation, then it is apparent that improved schooling has a crucially important part to play in the good society. The search is for an alternative to the existing system which will enhance freedoms, rights and duties.

RESEARCH

A research project based on the views of neo-critical theorists, might examine the sense of powerlessness and alienation that people may feel as they lose control of their own aspirations. The research might attempt to reveal those factors which hinder people from becoming effective autonomous beings, so that changes could be made through relevant policy. The private world of the individual in their arenas of social activity, in families and in schools, is open to ethnographic types of research. The power of the public world is that of the economic and technological, which exert increasing powers of control over the private world. The danger is that the State may come to dominate, hence the importance of education, language and communication to engender ideas which can be debated and on which agreement can be reached.

Points of evaluation
- Harbermas provides an optimistic view of human progress and social innovation and change as people reach understanding both with each other and of their society.
- If people can become enlightened as to the forces which control them and develop the skills and insights to combat them, they will become emancipated; the world in which people spend their schooling, as well as their leisure and work time, will be more under their control and open to change.
- For some critics, his arguments are not sufficiently critical of the aspects of capitalism which he recognises as a potentially dangerous colonising force, in the way that earlier critical and conflict theorists were.

POST-STRUCTURALISM

Post-structuralists reject the claim that there are any significant underlying structures (such as class background) which shape behaviour. They argue that the surface world, what we see and know, is all there is and this must be the subject of study. To understand why some children fail to make sense of the information provided by teachers, may lead us to examine the ways in which people can understand the social world from the information (or discourses) they receive. They do not see children shaped in their educational responses by economic structures or powerful hidden forces which control them like a puppet master. Instead, they would examine the world as it is experienced. Children who cannot make sense of their teacher's accent or method of presentation, because it is alien to that which they do understand, and the tones in which demands are normally made, or who find the material they have to learn as 'correct' knowledge, clashes with that they take for granted, may begin to fall behind. Furthermore, the discourse of the classroom may be abstract and conceptual, rather than concrete. But the post-structuralist warns that there can be no certainty about gaining objective knowledge of the causes of educational failure.

Study point

The reason why some students abandon a sociology course is because they cannot make sense of the ideas they are presented with when they clash with their ingrained presumptions about how and why people behave as they do. Do you agree?

RESEARCH

Davies (1989) utilised a post-structuralist perspective to examine the ways in which young children experienced difficulty in comprehending the significance of feminist endings to stories, in which the female showed dominance, because they challenged their existing understanding of male and female roles.

Critics of this approach complain that it takes insufficient account of the wider economic and political issues which shape the day to day life in a school, or other institution. They argue that ideas of post-structuralists (and postmodernists) have appeal because they are complex and only a small elite can handle them.

REALISM

Layder and **Clarke** (1994) have advocated a new realist approach in sociology to overcome the traditional divisions. This would concentrate on the nature of society as a whole, accept the significance of face to face encounters; and also search for underlying causes. They argue that what is required is more than a synthesis of positivism and interpretivism; realism seeks to discover and explore social processes that are not immediately observable.

RESEARCH

They explain that in adopting this approach a researcher would examine the underlying reasons that produce observable events. They might wish to know how the meanings and values of early school leavers are related to the wider social structure. They attempt to develop models of the causal processes at work beneath the surface of events; these would include ideological issues and how these intersect with other cultural resources in wider society.

POSTMODERNISM

This approach is similar to that of post-structuralism in that it also questions the idea that certain truths can be uncovered about social life. Everything is open to question.

Activity
Usher and **Edwards** (*Postmodernism and Education*, 1994) explain that 'there is a breakdown of the faith in science and rationality;' and 'in the condition of postmodernity there is a questioning of the modernists belief in a legitimating centre upon which beliefs and actions can be grounded...it is a world of rapid change, of bewildering instability, where knowledge is constantly changing and meaning floats without...belief in inevitable human progress.' Write this out in your own words.

Consequently, there is a constant process of change and restructuring which makes relationships, economies, moralities and cultures fluid and relative. Theories which claim absolute knowledge (such as Marxist conflict theories) are open to constant criticism.

POSTMODERN ANALYSIS OF EDUCATION

Criticisms

For the postmodernists the formal education system is open to a number of criticisms. They would not only question the possibility of teaching 'certain truths' about the scientific or social world to children, since knowledge is constantly being reassessed; they would also disapprove of the idea of imposing a universal national curriculum through which such material is presented. They would argue that its inflexibility will lead to its failure, since the school population is highly fragmented in terms of needs, abilities and intellectual development.

Higher education

The postmodernist would see the changes in higher education, in which there is greater fragmentation and flexibility in the ways in which they deliver their curriculum, as evidence of the development of a postmodern society. The old ideas of a rigid structure in which students in special institutions attended set lectures in specific departments at set times is changing.

Distance learning

This concept is entirely in keeping with trends in a postmodern society. A mature person may wish to train as a teacher, having not been involved in education since leaving school many years before. They may now be able to study at times suitable to themselves, in places they choose, perhaps close to their homes; courses are offered on a flexible and modular basis. Learners may be given credit for small steps they achieve. If they give up for a while they can pick up later, somewhere else on a transferable credit system and continue. Distance learning was paved by the Open University, with quality standards.

- A person may wish to change careers and not have the money to attend a traditional university.
- Local colleges might offer courses; but there are other sources from which degrees and diplomas can be obtained from a home base.

The decision was taken in 1999 to rule out a new University of Hereford, centralising study on a single purpose-built campus. Instead, education advisers recommended the development of a 'federal' option, with closer links between existing colleges and the promotion of tele-tutoring and video-conferencing as alternatives to traditional lectures. Such projects are already in place in the Highlands and Islands and the Genesis Project in Cumbria. The aim is to offer more part-time opportunities for learning, work-based learning and links with the private sector to provide new flexibility for older students and employers. In Herefordshire courses will include green crafts, sustainable land management, landscape architecture, heritage studies, adventure tourism and rural recreation. The 'university' will be guided by the postmodern ideal of experiential and lifelong learning. Local firms have indicated that they welcome new local HE facilities, with flexible timetabling, particularly in information technology and new product and process development. In the same way, the old system of grant funding for students has changed in modern society, another part of the fragmentation process of postmodern society. There are now various alternative sources to which people can apply.

RESEARCH IMPLICATIONS

Since there is in postmodernist approaches an implicit breakdown in faith in scientific and rational methods, it is difficult to promote any particular methodology for research purposes. However, **Usher and Edwards** argue that central to understanding contemporary economic, social and educational changes is the increased legitimacy given to conceptions of experiential learning (the use of experience as a resource for learners). This is especially celebrated as a gain for adult learners, in giving value to the learning that takes place outside of formally structured education and training opportunities.

Study point
Explain why experiential learning is part of the postmodern agenda.

These debates have been most influential in post secondary schooling, although they have come under attack when adopted in some junior and secondary schools as the possible cause of 'falling standards' since there is a lack of structure.

From the postmodern perspective, the themes are a challenge to more traditional sociological approaches. There is an emphasis on:

- The relativity of knowledge, from all sources, including that derived from popular culture. There are no right or wrong types of learning. Our knowledge and understanding of history and the present are relative, depending on the meanings we take
- There is an end to the grand theories of the past which endeavoured to provide all embracing explanations. To try and gather empirical data is misguided. The single snapshot they may provide is open to different interpretation providing a range of knowledge, rather than a single truth.

Points of evaluation

Those who favour the postmodernist arguments claim:

- This approach coincides with major changes in society in the new millennium. There are changes in higher and further education which encourage people to pick and mix courses, programmes and modules over time and place.
- There is a strong emphasis on the need for sociologists to feel that all research programmes have a validity. Consequently, new areas previously under-researched (or ignored) have opened up. In a school or college environment, these include the sociology of friendship, the sociology of food and eating, and the sociology of body image.
- The postmodernist has an optimistic view of the concept of experience. **Westwood** (1991) notes that the postmodernist has partly arisen from and provided space for the struggles of women, minority ethnic groups and homosexuals to be recognised.

Activity
Undertake a short study to see how far there has been a breaking down of barriers between high and popular culture, art and everyday life, as postmodernists predict.

Critics complain that :

- Without an objective standard, no judgements can be made about the worth of particular values or experiences. The really significant factor in affecting the way children respond to school, and teachers to pupils, is that of social class which continues to produce massive social inequalities.
- The proponents have attempted to destroy existing grand theories, and have succeeded in merely presenting another grand edifice which only serves to justify political inertia.
- For **Gellner** (1991) it is 'a kind of hysteria of subjectivity' whereas scientific methods provide 'external, objective, culture transcending knowledge.' He adds 'it is deterministic and anti-humanistic..'

STRUCTURATION

The work of **Giddens** makes extensive use of Piaget's concept of structuration, which represents another attempt to show how it is possible to combine perspectives to produce a richer analysis of social behaviour. His views oppose the relativist views of postmodernists.

He has said that for him, sociology is the study of the connections between individual lives and larger social forces. It is concerned with the impact of modernity on the world. By this, he means the condition of society from the period dating from the seventeenth century, known as the Enlightenment, to the middle of the twentieth. The modernity project is marked by the attempt to categorise and classify according to scientific principles, which it was claimed, produced certain knowledge about the world. Different disciplines emerged, such as natural sciences, chemistry, physics, biology, and social sciences including psychology and sociology. Each one initially adopted these principles so that there was progress in gaining a more complete understanding of the forces driving the natural and social world.

He suggests that the social world is made and remade through what we do in our everyday activities. In education, for example, children know the rules which must be obeyed to create the order and predictability required; they are active agents and through their interactions make sense of their world. They can just as easily disrupt it by choosing to undermine the teachers and oppose the values they promote.

RESEARCH

A structuration approach to research concerned with the relationship between social change and childhood would involve analysis of factors operating both inside and outside the school which affect attitudes and patterns of behaviour. For example, in a study entitled *Children 5–16: Growing into the 21st Century*, the issues the researchers examined were children as

- Economic actors discovering what they understand about employment and consumption; systems of benefit and how all these things affect their health, welfare and educational progress.
- As consumers of services discovering how much information they have about services available to people in society, and the experiences they have of them).
- As social actors (ie what their views and experiences are of parents, relatives and teachers and how they perceived their communities and the schools within them.
- As users and contributors to their physical environment how they are affected by different environmental and global experiences.

Such a study makes use of a range of research techniques and provides children with the chance to express opinions and views and draw on their experiences and those of teachers and parents.

FEMINISM

The disadvantages which girls experienced within the educational system became the focus of attention for many feminist writers from the 1970s. They wished to know the causes and consequences of an educational structure which produced differences based on gender. Feminism is an analytical perspective with a special agenda for its focus of research, methodologies for which may involve a range of techniques. These may include small-scale ethnographic studies to nationwide statistical surveys. There are a variety of perspectives used by feminists.

- **Marxist and socialist feminist** writers argue that the oppression of women is located in the economic capitalism of the twentieth century. The school is used to reproduce the relations of production found in wider society. Women are socialised to accept inferior roles.
- **Radical feminists** have focused more on events within the school, its organisation, culture and assumptions. Researchers taking this view have found that knowledge taught reflects male assumptions about the significance of men in the culture; the power of science (against intuition); the role of men as managers; the fact that boys achieve more highly in the 'important subjects' than girls who are frequently marginalised in the classroom; they tend to have less rewarding occupational careers than men.
- **Liberal feminists** have taken a more campaigning stance to the education of girls, drawing attention of teachers and heads to potential problems of discrimination in the classroom and in the school. Some of the outcomes have been opportunities for girls to play football and cricket, schemes to develop the interests of girls in science, and to ensure that boys are involved in home economics and made aware of issues of equality of opportunity.

Study point
Are discussions about equality of opportunity enough or are more radical changes needed in the educational system. Are single sex schools a possible answer?

• **Black feminist** writers emphasise that racism may be a more significant factor in affecting the outcomes of the educational experiences of many black girls, than sexism.

Gillborn (1995) has suggested that teachers work with stereotypes and that their expectations of black children include the view that they will be potentially disruptive. A form of self-fulfilling prophecy develops in which they are disciplined more frequently. This leads to increased negative perceptions on the part of teachers and a sense of defeat by the child, who begins to lose interest. This is used as evidence that they need to be disciplined more frequently for inattention and misbehaviour. In addition to racism on the part of other pupils and teachers, they are also faced with a largely Eurocentric curriculum, exacerbated by the national curriculum.

Points of evaluation
There is a danger of overgeneralising from this perspective and assuming high levels of failure among black children. There is some evidence that some black pupils do resist the stereotypical images and rather than become defeated by them, seek to disprove them by their efforts and academic successes. Success rates among some minority groups are better than those of their white contemporaries (see Chapter 9).

NEW RIGHT

The term New Right has arisen since the time of the Thatcher administrations and that of President Reagan in the USA during the 1980s. The values embody traditional Conservative principles, the minimal use of state intervention, the extension of the market economy and the concept of freedom of choice; the expansion of a variety of educational institutions to cater for the range of abilities and aptitudes which children display (see also Chapter 2).

RESEARCH IMPLICATIONS

Herrnstein and Murray (1994) see socio-economic differences between black and white pupils arising from differences in intelligence, which are the result of genetic factors. Much research is based on the use of what are considered to be objective intelligence tests to identify the most able pupils for whom more resources are advocated.

Marsland (1987) was a study undertaken by the author to examine an array of teaching materials because of his anxieties about the apparent one-sidedness of many introductory sociology textbooks. He expressed the view that 'the free market, pursuit of profit and competition are the central and indispensable mechanisms in the successful operation of liberal capitalist societies. Yet all three are either neglected or one-sidedly denigrated in sociology'. He therefore analysed their content to see whether there were expressions of anti-capitalist mentality. It was his finding that there was bias and that:

---

it was time for sociologists ...to throw off the self-imposed blinkers of an anti-capitalist bias...this done, we might have at last a sociology of freedom such as truth, genuine education, and Britain's social needs all demand.

Points of evaluation

- Whilst intelligence tests have become more sophisticated, those used by education psychologists examine a range of abilities and not one fixed quality.
- They became discredited as instruments for determining a child's educational potential and the work of one of the leading proponents, Sir Cyril Burt, was found to have been open to serious question. Some of his statistical analyses were unreliable; many were also culturally biased.
- It was also argued that they became a political tool useful for those on the political Right to justify systems of schooling they favoured.
- Marsland is equally critical of those who fail to present a balanced view of modern capitalist society, in textbooks; but may overlook the fact that students are perceptive and any kind of attempt to introduce bias (from whichever ideological perspective), may actually have an inoculating effect, causing rejection and suspicion.

Activity
Interview a sample of sociology students to see whether they believe they have been subject to bias in the presentation of material about the society in which they live. Have their political views been changed by studying sociology?

SUMMARY

The traditional perspectives have tended to produce an either/or approach to research in relation to education. Ethnographic research (participant observation) contrasted with the more scientific methods of functionalist and conflict theorists. Newer approaches which made use of a variety of research techniques, argue the need to produce a holistic view of the ways in which the educational system operates. The aim is to take account of the complexities of schooling at the end of the twentieth century in a time of rapid social and economic change. Postmodernists and poststructuralists claim that sociologists must adopt new methods, and take broader, more flexible views of the educational systems they study. Others advocate the need to watch, record, listen, ask questions, even make use of the insights of novelists, playwrights and other kinds of literature to aid understanding of social behaviour. Davis has said: 'the equivalent anomie story of Durkheim is, perhaps, The Great Gatsby. A good piece of work in family sociology...is O'Neill's Long Day's Journey into Night...A fine story on the meaning of vocation, as Weber would have analysed it, is the Thomas Mann short story Tonio Kroger.'

All insights from whatever sources may be valuable.

STUDY GUIDE

Group Work

1   Divide into postmodernists and anti-postmodernists. Consider the arguments for and against the idea that schooling should include emphasis on learning through experience, not just via a specialist curriculum. For example, spending days in art galleries, in museums, in the company of older people for discussions on philosophy, music, religion and politics.

Coursework Suggestions

1   Are students in the institution in which you study are more enlightened as to the factors which affect educational outcomes, the significance of different language codes and the implications of political ideologies than students studying other disciplines.

2 Devise a study which makes use of observation techniques, statistical data and interviews. For example, how far are pupils aware of the influence of school subcultures on their behaviour.to what extent are they associated with class differences?

Exam Tips

1 As you read a question do not dismiss it until you have re-read it.
2 Make clear answer plans for essay questions; avoid writing at excessive length.
3 Define key terms; control style and timing.

Revision Tips

1 Revise two or three topics at the same time to see their connections.
2 Continuous revision and consolidation ensures that work done at the start is not forgotten.
3 Most successful candidates put in the most classroom time and work to the most regular revision programmes.

Practice Questions

1 Education is less about learning through experience than learning for qualifications from books. Discuss this view.
2 The sociology of education faces the same problems as sociology in general: it needs to develop a single unified perspective. Discuss.
3 Sociologists who investigate children's performances in school must make use of a variety of methods to reach satisfactory accounts and explanations. Discuss.

7

FACTORS AFFECTING EDUCATIONAL PERFORMANCE

Introduction

THIS CHAPTER EXAMINES issues relating to why particular groups of children tend to be less successful in the educational system than others. Sociologists have examined the effects of factors outside the school, including home background, family value system, neighbourhood and wider economic influences. They have also studied factors within the school itself; the structure and organisation of educational institutions, effects of streaming or setting; expectations and perceptions of teachers; peer pressures and differences in the use of language.

Table 7: *Key Authors, Concepts and Issues in this Chapter*		
KEY AUTHORS	KEY CONCEPTS	KEY ISSUES
Lawson and Garrod Willmott and Young Jackson and Marsden Douglas	Social class	Class values on school attitudes Studies which illustrate the ways that class values operate
Westergaard Reid Kerkhoff and Trott	Social inequality	The potency of class in the 1990s Statistical data supports this view Class inequalities favour the high-status children
Wedge and Prosser Bordieu	Born to fail Cultural capital	Analysis of cultural disadvantages Disadvantages of poor parental education

Douglas	Home environment	Analysis of factors arising from birth order, family size
Bernstein Rosen Labov	Language codes	Analysis of use of language Critical response Strengths of working-class codes
Milson Brown	Peer groups	Analysis of peer-group types Analysis of peer pressures
Keddie	Streaming	Analysis of effects of streaming on teacher perceptions
Hargreaves	Labelling	Analysis of labelling processes
Meighan Rosenthal and Jacobson	Hidden curriculum Teacher expectation	The unintended ways in which the teacher's views are communicated Experiment to see how teacher's expectations affected performance
Lemert Renolds	Deviant	Processes by which label of deviant is confirmed Process by which some schools produce more deviants than others
Goldstein; Thomas; Sammons; Daly; Brown	School effectiveness	Studies since 1990 which examine differences in school effectiveness
Hutchinson and Whitehouse	Implementing change	Problem identified to assist processes of change
Hammersley and Turner Hopkins	Teacher attitudes	Some teachers shown to have positive attitudes towards less able Some recent policies have been supportive of teachers
Kohl	Teachers as victims	Analysis of constraints on teacher
Makins Maizels Slavin Blishen Veldman and Peck	Pupil perceptions Teaching styles Classroom constraints Pupil perceptions	Positive views of young children Negative views of older children Analysis of teacher effectiveness Pupils' need for a stimulating environment A valid source of data
Brake Hebdidge	School subcultures	Significance of style, especially for the more disaffected Cultures hold less relevance for those who can cope

FACTORS OUTSIDE THE SCHOOL

SOCIAL CLASS

Lawson and Garrod define social class as the hierarchical divisions of a capitalist society, in which wealth, income and occupation form the defining characteristics of each group. Statistically, members share similar lifestyles and life chances. They have differential access to the scarce resources of society, such as wealth, property, income, health and education and related services. The class structure which is a key form of stratification is frequently based on the Registrar General's Classification of Occupations.

Life chances describes the probability of a person achieving goals or suffering a social disadvantage; it provides the answer to the question 'who gets what'. Much sociological research in the 1950s and 60s showed that there were major differences in ideological value systems between middle- and working-class people. In particular studies by **Willmott and Young**, (1957); **Jackson and Marsden**, (1962); **Douglas** (1971) concluded that the social-class differences in educational opportunity which were considerable at the primary stage increased at the secondary. These and subsequent studies illuminate the varied aspects of social life in which class values play a significant part.

However, changing levels of prosperity in the 1980s and 90s caused some sociologists to question whether class remained a useful concept in analysis. **Westergaard** (1996) argues strongly that the potency of class had grown over the past 15 years or so, not diminished. Power had been increasingly concentrated at the top. He saw a concentration of upper class power and privilege.

Reid (1996) asks if there is any justifiable reason why the educational performance of one group in society should be superior to that of another. He accepts the earlier view of **Tawney** (1931) that the mark of a civilised society should be the aim of eliminating inequalities that have their source not in individual differences but in its own organisation. Table 10 shows that in 1991–2 the proportion of people with higher education qualifications (above A level) dropped across the classes from 78 per cent to 1 per cent. In the same way the proportion having no qualifications ranged from 3 per cent in Class 1 to 74 per cent in Class 6.

Table 8: *showing proportion of people with qualifications above A level 1991–2*

Class 1	Class 2	Class 3	Class 4	Class 5	Class 6
78	35	30	9	5	1
3	17	19	40	56	74

Source: General Household Survey 1992

Kerkhoff and Trott (1993) argued that class inequalities continue to provide advantage to those with high-status backgrounds so that differences in attainment at age seven continued to increase at 11 and until school leaving age. This suggests that despite policies to raise standards, those attempts at producing more egalitarian policies had so far failed. The social culture which people learn and which varies between classes can be seen in terms of two concepts: **cultural deprivation** and **cultural difference**.

CULTURAL DEPRIVATION

Wedge and Prosser (1973) compared the progress of all British children born in a single week in March 1958. It found that nearly 900,000 children were growing up disadvantaged at that time. They faced an accumulation of problems which made their future prospects bleak. The study compared the lives of the disadvantaged minority when they were aged 11 with the rest. The research revealed:

- One in four was growing up in a family with five or more children or with only one parent in bad housing (family density of more than one person per room, or no hot water for the exclusive use of the family)
- One in seven was in a low income family (based on nationally applied means tests and benefits)
- One in 16 suffered all three disadvantages
- By the age of 11 the disadvantaged group were three and a half years behind their peers in reading ability.

The outcomes were less healthy children who underachieved in school; had behaviour problems and poor outcomes on leaving school. They were subject to a cycle of deprivation which, for many, was passed on from one generation to the next. Attempts to remedy these problems among lower working class children resulted in programmes of compensatory education and other special policy schemes, such as Headstart (in the USA), Educational Priority Areas and Educational Action Zones in Britain.

CULTURAL DIFFERENCE THEORY

This suggests that working class children are more likely to underachieve in school because there is a mismatch between the cultural values of the home and those of the school. Children develop different attitudes, values and ways of behaving and expressing themselves arising from their socio-economic class backgrounds. Some broad distinctions were suggested by **Lockwood and Goldthorpe** (1960) as distinguishing the typical lower working class value system from that of middle class professionals. Wheras the former were fatalistic, the latter emphasized qualifications and personal initiative for success.

Many observers still argue that those children who are socialised into values of ambition, and who receive parental support are more likely to achieve success. This helps account for their higher levels of educational achievement. It is argued that the reverse is true for children from lower-working-class homes. This is the basis of the views of **Bordieu** (1974) who has argued that each class possesses its own cultural framework which informs members about tastes, values and behaviour. Each class has varying amounts of cultural capital. Those with greatest amounts, inherited from their home background, will be judged to be the most able. In this way the school reproduced existing patterns of social inequality. His work is criticised because:

- It is presented from a Marxist framework of analysis, which assumes a ruling class domination of the educational system and its curriculum.
- There are many examples of working class children who lacked cultural capital but who subsequently achieved great success and power. John Major, the Prime Minister 1990–97 is one such person.

Reid concludes that social inequalities in education, together with those caused by and through education, persist in Britain in the 1990s. To tackle them it would require either increased or redistributed resources, accurately targeted. There is evidence that economic inequality grew in Britain between 1979 (when 10 per cent of children were living in households whose incomes were less than half the national average) and 1992 (when the figure had risen to 32 per cent). He advocates positive discrimination towards the most disadvantaged, who need extra, exclusive opportunities.

Points of evaluation

Critics of the significance of cultural difference theory have noted that:

- It is hard to specify the extent of parental interest in a child's work in school. The working-class parent who attends frequently to complain may be defined as a nuisance; the middle-class parent may be seen as 'showing interest'.
- The less frequent attendance of working-class parents at school events, may reflect the nature of their work, which may entail late shifts.
- Furthermore, the child is also shaped by events within the school; poor reports or negative labelling may deter effort to improve. Their careers can be said to be constructed as much by the school as by the home.
- There may be a danger in assuming that attitudes are learned in a deterministic way, which take the child down an inevitable path. Attitudinal differences alone cannot explain educational differences in attainment.

THE HOME

POSITION IN THE FAMILY

Douglas (1967) argued that the position in the family may be significant. He found that eldest children tended to receive more parental involvement in early years and the stimulus of the presence of a younger child in the family. This had an effect in their secondary education. Boys, in particular, showed higher levels of aspiration than their younger siblings.

Douglas, et al (1971) noted that pupils from two-child families with birth intervals of two to four years made higher scores in all tests than those with either shorter or longer intervals. He also found that children from large families produced lower scores in attainment tests at all ages, although there was no evidence of increasing educational disadvantage at secondary school. But the more young children there were in the family when a child was learning to talk the lower the score in the eight-year-old vocabulary test, a deficiency not made up later.

LINGUISTIC DEVELOPMENT

Bernstein (1972) suggested that patterns of language varied significantly between social class groups. The more middle-class children show evidence of a richer language code than working-class children.

The middle-class use of language was:

- More abstract
- More elaborate and specific
- More grammatically correct.

The working-class code was:

- More restricted (limited vocabulary)
- More concrete and descriptive
- Grammatically simple with many technical errors in usage.

He argues that the restricted code is inadequate in formal education. The elaborated code enables more complex and abstract ideas to be expressed. Whereas the middle-class child can make use of both codes, one in the playground and one in the classroom, the working class child is at an educational disadvantage in using only the restricted code, especially as far as examination success is concerned.

Points of evaluation
Rosen (1974) criticised the use of the terms *elaborated* and *restricted*.

- They may imply a qualitative difference between the classes themselves.

- Teachers may come to see working class children as ineducable.
- He argues that working class speech has its own strengths and it is wrong to see it as 'deformed' or 'under-powered.'

Labov (1973) also denies that working-class children cannot express complex ideas. His analysis of the language patterns of black working class children showed a rich verbal culture; the children themselves also showed a capacity for complex conceptual learning.

REGIONAL FACTORS

Repeated studies have shown regional variations in educational opportunities and variations in performance of children in schools.

(i)   The Born to Fail? study showed that:

- One child in 47 in the south of England was disadvantaged; in Wales and northern England it was one in every 12.
- In Scotland it was one in 10. There, 11 per cent of 11-year-old British children were living and 19 per cent were disadvantaged.

Disadvantaged children have been shown to live in poorer accommodation than those who are successful in school and more live in inner city areas. They are less likely to have access to indoor play centres, clubs and other leisure facilities. They make less use of public libraries.

(ii)   *DES Study* 1984 examined the attainments of pupils in English LEAs comparing 16 and 18+ performances on the basis of the percentage of pupils living in households whose heads had non-manual occupations (Classes 1 and 2). A strong relationship was identified between those who obtained five or more high grade exam passes and their social background which varied between regions. Better results were obtained by those in the most prestigious areas.

PEER INFLUENCE

A peer group consisting of a small circle of close friends or age-mates is generally based on age, sex, social class and shared interests. Socialisation is the process whereby individuals learn and absorb the relevant values, norms and patterns of behaviour. They learn their social roles. As developing young people they assume a role repertoire. The peer group is important as a source of support, friendship and a more specific identity. One of the demands is that members should conform to the group's norms and values, or be rejected.

Therefore, to be influenced by the norms of an anti-school culture will affect achievement levels.

Milson (1972) has identified a typology of peer groups.

- The conformists: who adopt and conform to the dominant norms of society; the majority.
- The experimenters: who become personal or political revolutionaries; they develop a lifestyle which disengages from what is seen as acceptable social goals of success and ambition.
- The deprived: who adopt attitudes of rejection, anti-social values.

The values of the family may be undermined by the values of the peer group, especially during adolescence when peer relations become more intense, complex and exclusive of adults.

Brown (1982) found that adolescents reported significantly stronger peer pressure to spend time with peers than to participate in activities related to family or school.

INTELLIGENCE: HEREDITY OR ENVIRONMENT

Many attempts have been made to measure intelligence. Binet devised tests in 1905 to measure mental age and Terman produced an index of mental development:

$$\text{Intelligence Quotient (IQ)} = \left. \frac{\text{mental age}}{\text{actual age}} \right\} \times 100$$

There were constant attempts in the 1930s and 40s to relate intelligence (as measured by the tests they devised) to social class. Some held a view that intelligence was a matter of heredity, passed from parents to children, to account for the fact that children from lower social classes performed less well in school than those from professional backgrounds. Many sociologists examined the issue to see the influence of environmental factors.

Table 9: *Entry to Grammar Schools (data from two local education authorities) 1965*

	CLASS 1 PROFESSIONAL	CLASS 2 WHITE COLLAR	CLASS 3 CLERICAL	CLASS 4 SKILLED	CLASS 5 SEMI-SKILLED	CLASS 6 UNSKILLED
% PASSED 11+	54	39	18	22	8	2
% IN THE CLASS WHO FAIL	46	61	82	78	92	98

Source: Swift (1965) quoted in Meighan

This showed that children from Classes 1 and 2, the middle class sector, produced the greatest proportion of successful entrants; those from Classes 5 and 6 very few representatives. Grammar school entry was clearly related to father's occupation. The 11+ test used after the 1944 Education Act to select for grammar school entry was eventually agreed to be flawed.

- It was culturally biased in favour of middle class children (they could score more highly because they were more likely to be familiar with some of the question areas and for which they were more likely to be coached).
- The tests did not measure potential for future ability, only a snapshot picture of differences in ability on one particular day between children.
- An IQ gene has never been identified.
- The tests tend to measure a capacity to conform to the tester's restrictions. Only the test maker's answer is correct. They ignored creativity and imaginative skills.
- It was argued that a child's future should not be based on the results of an unreliable test.
- Knowledge of test score results by teachers may affect the ways they treat the child in the classroom.
- The system led to social divisions and a loss of talent among a large proportion of the school population, who were regarded as less able and given fewer opportunities to obtain qualifications. This led to the development of comprehensive education. In the year 2000 163 grammar schools remain in existence.

In 1963 the *Robbins Report* showed 63 per cent of respondents from Class 1 had a degree compared to 1 per cent in the lowest classes. Data for 1992–3 shows little change in this regard.

Table 10: *Educational qualifications by social class (1993)*			
	PROFESSIONAL	SEMI-SKILLED	UNSKILLED
Degree	61	2	
Higher edn.	16	4	2
A level	7	7	3
GCSE A–C	7	21	12
GCSE D–E	1	12	10
No qualification	3	51	70

Source: Household Survey 1994

RESOURCE PROVISION

The level of educational provision available to schools varies between LEAs. The amounts spent on buildings, equipment and other facilities correlates with attainment levels in schools. The higher the resource expenditure the higher the achievement levels and the greater the life chances of children in those areas.

Points of evaluation
The attitudes of parents, their cultural background and the ability of their children are inter-related. The evidence does point to the fact that the experience of being brought up in a middle-class home and neighbourhood gives advantages in coping with educational institutions; those suffering multiple deprivation in lower-class groups being especially prone to educational failure. A network of causes outside the school is perhaps the most useful way of explaining differences in educational attainment, when taken in conjunction with factors internal to the school itself.

FACTORS AFFECTING PERFORMANCE INSIDE THE SCHOOL

STRUCTURE, VALUES AND INTERACTIONS WITHIN THE SCHOOL

Sociologists who make an analysis of what happens inside a school generally work at a micro level, although increasingly attempts are being made to utilise a range of methods which take account of the complex interrelationships of factors (see Chapter 6).

TEACHER-PUPIL RELATIONS

Pupils as victims
Many studies suggest that the development of pupils within the educational setting may be affected by several factors beyond their control. These include the effects of teacher expectation and the policies relating to streaming.

Streaming
Keddie (1971) says that sociologists must examine the meanings which lie beneath what counts as knowledge in the classroom, and discover the methods

by which teachers evaluate a child's ability. These included their use of language; consequently more middle-class children appeared in the highest sets or streams. Those from working-class homes tended to present knowledge and ideas in more concrete ways, which was less highly valued. They filled the lower streams. Teachers then were found to modify their methods and approaches according to the stream they were teaching. Those with highest status were considered more able to deal with highly evaluated knowledge. Pupils, in turn, responded to the teacher in terms of the stream in which they were placed; those in the A group more willing to accept the teacher's methods and that the knowledge they received was valid. Attitudes differed in lower streams, where pupils were more likely to dispute, criticise and disrupt. This gives rise to issues of labelling, based on the teacher's knowledge of the pupils gathered in the process of classroom evaluation.

Labelling theory

Hargreaves et al (1975) observed teachers to see how they made sense of pupil behaviour, ability and potential. They found that they classified them as they got to know them. They went through a process which entailed a speculative hypothesis about what they seemed to be like. Gradually these were made more specific and hardened into what they took to be their knowledge of each child. They took into account their social background; their classroom manners; their personalities; their social skills with other staff and children and information provided in the staffroom from colleagues. In this way it became more elaborated; stabilisation occurred as the assumptions became confirmed by observation and colleague agreement. All related patterns of behaviour become understandable and predictions can be made about future prospects. These may be positive and encouraging or negative and dispiriting. In some cases, it has been argued they can lead to increased deviant activity, if the label is accepted by the pupil.

The hidden curriculum and self-fulfilling prophecies

The expectations of teachers are a factor in the operation of the hidden curriculum. **Meighan** notes how: 'The teacher's prediction of a pupil's or a group of pupils' behaviour is held to be communicated to them, frequently in unintended ways, thus influencng the actual behaviour that follows.'

These may become sources of false prediction and often self-fulfilling prophecies. They are based on misjudgements relating to gender, ethnicity, religion, name, handwriting, physical appearance, dress and social-class indicators, especially speech. All these become evident in the processes of social interaction. The pupil may develop a self-concept based on the knowledge of the teacher's perceptions and behave in accordance with it. This action is seized on by the teacher as evidence of the prediction, which is fulfilled.

Attempts to test the self-fulfilling prophecy have been undertaken, most notably by **Rosenthal and Jacobson** (1968). They claimed that teachers' expectations can significantly affect their pupils' performance levels, based on an experiment in which they fed false information to teachers about the ability level of a random sample of children. Those given the label of high ability pupils, were found to achieve better results a year later than others not so labelled. Whilst some criticisms have been made of the methodology used, the halo effect does seem to be a real one, although not inevitable and entirely predictable. The processes by which labels become attached and effective are complex.

THE STAFF AND THE HEADTEACHER

The ethos of the school, its values, organisation, administration and status in the community will have much to do with the headteacher and relationships with staff, governors and the local community.

The construction of deviant behaviour

Interactionists stress that the control exercised in a school by teachers can lead to deviant behaviour in pupils. The more rules which are created, the greater the number of rule breakers who will be identified. In some cases this behaviour will fit with prior expectations; where it does not, it may be perceived as less worthy of comment or sanction.

From this perspective, deviant behaviour in school is described as a social process which passes through several stages. The offence (which need not be breach of any legal rule) must be observed or acted on by a rule enforcer who is able to ensure that others (staff and pupils) are aware of the behaviour. The deviant label 'nuisance', 'troublemaker,' 'fool, ' 'clown' may not become fixed unless the person so labelled begins to accept it.

Lemert (1972) has said that the key issue is whether the primary deviant (the first time offender) becomes a secondary deviant, following further behaviour which attracts critical comment. The enforcement of stronger sanctions results in hostility on the part of the pupil, who acts in more deviant ways as a reaction to the criticisms; the deviant label is fixed.

Reynolds (1979) showed that schools which had the strongest policies of social control over pupils produced the greatest number of deviants. Schools which took a less stringent attitude over behaviour which was not a serious threat to the smooth running of the school, had fewest.

The more successful schools had certain things in common. They:

- Were smaller in size than less successful ones
- Had lower levels of staff turnover
- Had smaller classes
- Operated with older, more established buildings

- Were likely to have an effective prefect and pastoral care system
- Enforced school rules less vigorously and obsessively than less successful schools
- Did not use a harsh authoritarian mode of control

The conclusion was that where there are conflicts within the school, there will be vandalism within it and higher rates of delinquency outside it. The organisational style of the school is therefore an important influence on pupil behaviour.

Overall school effectiveness

Much research has been conducted in this area since 1988.

- **Goldstein et al** (1993) looked at stability over time of the effects on schools
- **Thomas et al** (1995) examined consistency of school effects on different outcomes (in terms of different subjects)
- **Sammons et al** (1993) studied the differential effects of school for different groups of students (for example of different ethnic or class backgrounds)
- **Daly** (1991) showed the existence of size of school on outcomes
- **Brown et al** (1996) researched labelling practices and teacher–pupil interactions in relation to special educational needs
- **Reynolds** (1996) undertook a study of classroom practices in ineffective schools.

Several factors have been shown to be potentially important in creating effectiveness. The most effective have:

(i) Strong relationships between head and deputy.

(ii) A management style involving heads setting appropriate academic and other target goals, establishing directions and possessing a clear mission statement and organisational cohesion and consistency.

(iii) The staff actively involved in planning the means of achieving goals, with strong supportive systems in place.

(iv) Enthusiastic and supportive parental involvement in all aspects of school work.

(v) A clear system of rewards for achievement and effort.

(vi) High levels of active pupil involvement inside and outside the classroom.

Problems of implementing changes

There is some evidence that some teachers may be resistant to changes recommended as a result of research or from reporting bodies.

Hutchinson and Whitehouse (1986) found entrenched attitudes (sometimes on the part of headteachers) among classroom teachers. One is quoted as saying: ' I will teach the way that suits me best, after all I've had long enough experience and nobody will tell me what or how I should be teaching.' Other research suggests that there will be some teachers who are keen to revise their methods.

Hammersley and Turner (1984) point out that some are very sympathetic to pupils with problems and have less empathy with the more able conformists they teach.

Hopkins (1996) states categorically that whilst there has been a great deal of change expected of teachers and schools since 1986, many of the policy initiatives have been potentially supportive of teachers and school development.

Teachers as victims

Kohl (1970) has suggested that both heads and teachers can be seen as victims. This view stresses the constraints that are imposed on them, especially in terms of the conditions of work.

- The Head receives a building, handed on from a predecessor
- The buildings often have an institutional atmosphere of a place not associated with pleasure; they are designed to inhibit individual or small group learning and democratic relationships
- Classrooms are like shop floors in factories; children are passed through processes of production according to certain criteria in specified groups and times and at regulation-sized desks
- Staff receive without much power of negotiation an external examination system for which they must prepare their students
- They are subject to the powers of a local bureaucracy, the education authority
- They must work to a specified timetable and follow a national curriculum precisely
- They may have no resources to support their work or they may reject such materials because they have not been trained to use them
- They may be faced with a headteacher whose ideology of education conflicts with their own, but which they must accept
- They may have disaffected pupils and difficult parents to work with.

The cumulative effect may be to make an ineffective teacher which undermines the opportunities for the children in that school. The teachers are forced into an authoritarian role, even against their better judgement. Their need to uphold school rules (which may be seen as petty and trivial) and to protect the school fabric (often of inferior design and quality) undermine a developing relationship between staff and pupils and make enjoyment of school less likely.

Hopkins (2000) says that to improve schools better teachers are needed, by encouraging them to become researchers in their own right and to base practice on solid research. He has established the National College for School Leadership which will train heads in new ways of running an efficient school. For him the aim is to create classrooms and schools where both children and teachers learn. He is calling for a new fluid and flexible system of school structures, with perhaps one visionary head in charge of a cluster of schools, each run by a super-deputy.

PUPIL–TEACHER RELATIONSHIPS

There has not been much research which examines the school from the pupil's perspective. There is a suggestion from some, however, that most pupils can offer constructive suggestions for improvements, but they are seldom asked and few schools have effective pupil–teacher councils by which information could flow effectively between the consumers and the suppliers of education. The relationship with the teachers is especially significant, since they have control and influence over each child.

WHICH TEACHING STYLE DO YOU PREFER: AUTHORITARIAN; LIBERAL OR LAISSEZ-FAIRE?

Attitudes towards the teacher

Primary pupils appear to be more satisfied with their experiences of school than secondary pupils.

Makins (1969) analysed 1,200 responses from 11-year-old children who provided descriptions of their teachers. She describes the ways that they observed their teachers in great detail, their mood changes, mannerisms, special skills and patterns of behaviour. They showed a great enjoyment of school.

Maizels (1970) finds the reverse true in secondary schools. Only a minority of the sample showed much enthusiasm for school or for the teachers, who seldom displayed much enthusiasm or innovation in teaching methods. There were some constructive suggestions about how they could improve by making lessons more interesting and up to date.

Teaching styles

It is apparent that different styles of teaching suit different pupils. Some respond best to authoritarian approaches and others to more liberal or laissez-faire styles. The same pupils may show different behaviour patterns as they move from one classroom teacher to another. **Slavin** (1996) suggests that teacher effectiveness relates to:

* Clarity of presentation; appropriateness of task and management of the learning environment
* Restricted range of goals, with appropriate incentives and high expectations
* Questioning skills; appropriate grouping strategies and reward based control.

Constraints within a classroom

Blishen (1969) has noted that from the pupils' perspective, they would enjoy the opportunity to personalise their space (as much as headteachers do theirs): 'They cry out for colour...they would like to have some say in the ephemeral decoration of their schools; they long for attractive grounds, especially for trees.'

The conclusion is that many teachers show poor environmental competence and understanding of the significance of spatial influences on learning.

Points of evaluation

From a functionalist point of view the emphasis is on the school as a place of training in social skills. Children need to be moulded. This is a view held by those who control the institution as well as most of its employees. Consequently many heads and classroom teachers may object to pupils commenting on teachers and their methods:

* There would be dangers of pupils undermining the authority of the teacher
* Classroom relationships would deteriorate over time with frequent reporting
* Pupils would make irrational judgements without contextual references.

However, interactionists dispute these views.

Veldman and Peck (1963) suggested that the recorded perceptions of pupils was sufficiently reliable to be worth considering as evidence for teachers about their skills. Where this has been fed back, teachers found that previously obstructive children became more cooperative when their views were taken seriously.

Blishen (1969) supported these findings and also found that bad teachers were seen as those who were lazy, used fear to dominate, were moody and miserable. They were remote, often sarcastic, applied trivial rules, lacked sympathy and failed to admit ignorance or uncertainty. Many of these criticisms were associated with teachers having to follow specific syllabus documents and a constraining curriculum. In addition pupils favoured coeducational and comprehensive schools; disapproved of traditional classrooms which lacked imagination, assemblies, religious instruction, prefects, homework and the poor facilities for children.

Points of evaluation
The ways that pupils respond to their schooling is seldom taken into account. The traditional view is that pupils should not be consulted since they are consumers of a social provision; they would not be competent to make judgements and would undermine the position of the staff if they were to do so. However, there are findings which contradict this view; which suggests that a more participative relationship between pupil and teacher could result in less deviant behaviour.

PUPIL–PUPIL RELATIONSHIPS

School subcultures, related to streaming, setting or banding have been shown to develop. These arise from pupils perceiving their education in school in different ways in accordance with their experiences. Pupils with similar labels tended to relate closely, especially within age groups. The peer group carries the culture, through its shared appreciation of certain kinds of music, clothes and other aspects of wider youth culture.

(i) **Brake** (1985) suggested that such subcultures were 'meaning systems, modes of expression or life style developed by groups in subordinate structural positions in response to dominant meaning systems.' He presents an image of youth cultures as style, providing an alternative form of social reality. For those most disaffected by school attachment to a subculture, enables them to obtain more enjoyment, success and self esteem than they can through the formal rules of the classroom, where they may experience little of either.
(ii) **Hebdidge** (1979) describes a distinction between 'youth as trouble and youth as fun'. For pupils who can cope, subcultures may nonetheless figure in their lives, but to a less radical extent. For them it enables them to sideline the dominant culture which has little significance in their day-to-day lives and to share rituals symbolic of resistance; special words, ways of adapting school uniform and so on.

Points of evaluation
There is a danger in assuming that all pupils fit neatly into one type of classification or another, whereas attachment to cultural groups may fluctuate or have little significance other than as a source of shared interests in sport, television or social activities. They may become more relevant in an analysis of the behaviour of those pupils to whom deviant labels have been successfully attached.

SUMMARY

The analysis of the factors affecting educational performance, is complex. Some sociologists have focused on the cultural-deficit model. The deprivations and disadvantages within different class groups is emphasised and the negative influence of new policies. Attention is on the out-of-school factors:

- The cultural and socio-economic background from which a child comes
- Region and local environment
- Peers and subcultures (attitudes towards education).

Others have looked at in-school factors. For some commentators (conflict theorists) this model also points to deficiencies in the ways that educational outcomes continue to be patterned in terms of social class distinctions, reproduced in the ways that teachers perceive their pupils and act on their assumptions. For others (structural functionalists) there will be more positive interpretations, with the emphasis on the inevitability and functional necessity of inequality.

Attention is on:

- The variations in quality of schools
- Relationships between pupil–teacher and pupil–pupil
- The organisation of the school, its staff values, methods and its ethos.

STUDY GUIDE

Exam Tips

1 Keep to the technique which you have used in revision. If you have developed spider diagrams or other planning methods, use them.
2 Keep your concentration on the question in hand; avoid becoming distracted by making notes for another.
3 Don't start another question directly beneath the previous one, in case you wish to add to it.

Practice Questions

1 Assess the extent to which school factors explain differential educational achievement between social classes or ethnic groups.
2 To what extent do you agree that teachers' judgements of pupils are the main cause of underachievement in schools?
3 Cultural differences and disadvantages are more relevant in explaining under-achievement than what goes on in the school. Discuss.

8

GENDER AND EDUCATION

Introduction

THIS CHAPTER EXAMINES the ways in which educational attainment varies between genders; the nature of the inequalities which exist between them in relation to factors both outside and inside the school.

KEY AUTHORS	KEY CONCEPTS	KEY ISSUES
Reid	Educational inequalities	The significance of cultural and social factors in shaping attitudes
Saunders	Test score ability	The significance of test scores as predictors of career outcomes
Crompton and Sanderson	White-collar jobs	The effects of the sex-typing of jobs has not advantaged women
Hakim		Women should not be seen as victims
Cohen	Failing boys	The issues relating to boys' underachievement
Mahoney Jackson		A view of the wider social context Boys' underachievement is not a new problem
Murphy and Elwood	Gender preferences	Interests and skills learnt in the home transfer to the school
Barber	Educational disaffection	Related to the motivation to learn
Reed	Failing schools	There is a link between failing boys and failing schools
Hey	Special educational needs	Provision is dominated by males
Epstein	Successful girls	Girls remain less successful than boys in achieving top degrees

Table 11: Key Authors, Concepts and Issues in this Chapter

Abbott and Wallace (1997) explain that 'sex differences' refers to biological differences between males and females. 'Gender' is used as a way of understanding the cultural and social construction of roles appropriate to men and women.

EVIDENCE OF GENDER DIFFERENCES IN EDUCATIONAL ACHIEVEMENT

In 1963 it was shown that girls were severely disadvantaged within the educational system:

- Three times as many girls as boys left school at the earliest age (15)
- Only a third of A level students were girls
- Only a quarter of university students were female.

By 1973 girls were showing some improvements in their attainments. But females still took only 36 per cent of university places.

Meighan (1981) noted the regular pattern that appeared in the educational biographies of girls and boys in Britain until the early 1980s.

- Their achievements were found to be similar up to the age of 11.
- Although examination entries contained similar proportions, twice as many boys gained passes in science subjects; girls gained more passes in arts subjects.
- Ratios of boys to girls in various A level subjects showed that in physics it was 6:1, in mathematics 4:1, in chemistry 3:1, biology 9:8, and technical drawing 200:1.
- For every 100 boys leaving with one A level subject there were 90 girls.
- In 1978 62 per cent of boys and 38 per cent of girls gained places in universities. Even the Open University had more male than female students. However, more girls took up teaching training opportunities.
- 42 per cent of boys obtained apprenticeships on leaving school and only 7 per cent of girls.

In the 1980s and into the 1990s statistical data began to show that it was no longer the case that boys outperformed girls academically in a wide range of subjects; in fact the reverse was true. Nonetheless, the glass ceiling remained firmly in place in the work arena despite anti-discrimination legislation. However, whilst some significant changes did occur in the patterns of educational attainment, choice and outcomes, there have been some differentials which have remained entrenched. The picture is therefore more complex than before.

THE CHANGES 1985—99

Social Trends (1994) shows that the number of boys gaining 5 or more O/GCSE passes in 1985–6 was 10 per cent and girls 12 per cent. The DfEE report for 1999 showed that:

- 47 per cent of all pupils achieved 5 or more grades at GCSE or the GNVQ equivalent
- 88 per cent achieved at least 5 grades A–G
- 6 per cent failed to achieve a single pass
- Girls continued to outperform boys especially at the higher grades (A–C) 53 per cent of girls achieved at least 5 of these compared with 42 per cent of boys.
- Points average at A level: Girls: 18.2; boys: 17.8
- Girls were out-performing boys even at the age of 11

In 1999 statistics from the Department for Education and Employment showed that:

Table 12:		
% OF BOYS AND GIRLS ACHIEVING EXPECTED LEVEL IN READING AND WRITING AT AGE 11 (1998–99)		
AT AGE 11	% REACHING EXPECTED LEVEL IN READING	
	1998	1999
Girls	79%	84%
Boys	64%	78%
	% REACHING EXPECTED LEVEL IN WRITING	
Girls	61%	64%
Boys	45%	49%

Source: Dept. Education and Unemployment 1999

The evidence now points to the fact that at the end of the twentieth century:

- Girls were more successful, academically, than boys at every point in the national curriculum SATs, in maths, science and English.
- They out-performed boys in many of the major GCSE and A level subjects.
- 74 per cent of 16-year-old girls were in post-16 full-time secondary education and 68 per cent of males.
- 53 per cent of those accepted for university degree course were female; 47 per cent were male.

Nonetheless, some examination subjects are still more popular with girls than boys both at GCSE level and more so at A level. The most extreme examples are:

The reverse is true of other subjects:

Table 13:			
EXAM SUBJECTS	% EXAM ENTRIES	GIRLS	BOYS
Social studies	GCSE	67	33
Social sciences	A level	66	34
Communication	GCSE	54	46
studies	A level	64	36
Religious	GCSE	60	40
studies	A level	75	25
Music, drama,	GCSE	53	47
art	A level	61	39
Home	GCSE	89	11
economics	A level	95	5
Foreign	GCSE	53	47
languages	A level	68	32
English	GCSE	51	49
	A level	69	31

Table 14:			
EXAM SUBJECTS	% EXAM ENTRIES	GIRLS	BOYS
Craft, design and	GCSE	48	52
technology	A level	19	81
Computer studies	GCSE	39	61
and related	A level	16	84
mathematics	GCSE	49	51
	A level	35	65
Physics, chemistry	GCSE	37	63
and biology	A level	44	56

In others the numbers are more evenly balanced

Table 15:			
EXAM SUBJECTS	% EXAM ENTRIES	GIRLS	BOYS
Geography	GCSE	44	56
	A level	45	55
History	GCSE	51	49
	A level	55	45
Business studies	GCSE	45	55
	A level	47	53

Sources: DFEE (separate tables, 1997)

Quoted in *Sociology Review* Vol 8 No 1, 1998 (p 31)

THE IMPROVEMENTS IN GIRLS' ACHIEVEMENTS

The improved performances of females and the changes in relative levels of attainment in education between the genders has many possible explanations, which can be examined in terms of what has happened outside the school and within it over the past 20 years.

OUT-OF-SCHOOL FACTORS

Changing cultural attitudes

Veness (1962) showed that about 50 per cent of the sample of 600 girls saw marriage as their most likely 'job' by the age of 25. The girls had lower career ambitions than the boys and saw less value in academic qualifications. Similar results were found by later researchers.

Sharpe (1970) also noted how girls were steered towards domestic science, arts subjects, typing and related skills. Boys were encouraged more into sciences and technical subjects. She concluded that girls were limited in outlook by the power of existing attitudes and ideologies.

The influence of feminist writers

In the 1970s the Women's Liberation Movement developed with many writers beginning to point to the gender inequalities in society and identifying the causes. They focused on the patriarchal ideology which predominated within organizations and institutions in British society in which power was generally in male hands. Feminist writers argued that the issues of gender ideology ran through every aspect of social life. The work of feminists such as **Millett** (1970); **Greer** (1971); **Oakley** (1974); and others began to have an effect on the ways that girls perceived themselves, the attitudes of parents and of teachers. Their work was significant because they:

- Challenged the idea that biology determines destiny.
- Showed how differences in patterns of socialisation encouraged the view that some subjects and some jobs are more suitable for one gender than the other.
- Pointed out that the images of what is appropriate behaviour for boys and girls varies between societies and within societies over time.
- Argued that sociology needs this feminist approach to show how women are exploited in families and constrained in schools by traditional images.

They also showed how women were subjected to the ideology of femininity, which emphasises that the natural role of women is that of wife and mother. This dual ideology predominated and affected they ways in which women came to think about themselves, their abilities, attitudes to school and the value of qualifications and high-level careers. It helped determine the limits to their roles in wider society. Feminists argue that many changes subsequently occurred, which are reflected in improved educational attainments of girls.

Points of evaluation

There is evidence that many of the areas of concern to feminists have not fully disappeared.

(i) **Cockburn** (1999) shows that the stereotypical images of girls who enjoy competition and achievement as a male characteristic, may still affect girls' attitudes, especially towards sport and PE. Those who did take an interest in such activities often hid the fact because they felt it was a turn-off for boys.

(ii) The extent to which girls have overtaken boys in science subjects may depend how the statistics are interpreted. If results of a group of subjects are aggregated such as A level physics, chemistry, maths, computer studies, biology and home economics, then girls may have better pass rates because they are especially strong in the latter two subjects.

THE HOME AND FAMILY VALUES

Functionalists emphasise how the home remains a primary source of socialisation; with each generation of women improving their educational attainment, they are in a stronger position to assist and encourage their own daughters.

Feminists argue that parents typically treat boys differently from girls; feminine behaviour in sons is discouraged, whereas qualities of toughness, aggression and independence are favoured. In girls the qualities of kindness, helpfulness, sensitivity and gentleness have traditionally been valued. In this way children learn gender identity. It is reinforced through books, television, advertising and other images. The need to avoid sexist stereotyping became a major issue in the 1990s, which advertisers and journalists began to heed. This was assisted by legislation designed to prevent discrimination against women. However, although girls continue to improve their educational attainments, this is not necessarily reflected in career opportunities. Women with similar qualifications to men remain less likely to achieve the highest positions within an occupation. Neither are rates of pay always equal for the same job.

Walby (1990) explains this anomaly by arguing that women are still exploited in the economic world as they are in the family, which serves both the interests of the capitalist economic system and men. Males have their daily needs for care, love and affection and running of the household, serviced by unpaid female labour. This is a major feature of the ideology of the family which is largely taken for granted and goes unquestioned by many women. These values feed into the education system, and continue to influence the values of some girls, especially those with low levels of ambition or sense of worth. For some girls, there may still be the influences identified by **Sharpe** in the 1970s, which inhibit their opportunities to develop all their talents.

Points of evaluation
Phillips (1993) is critical of such feminists for developing dangerous values in young women; especially the rejection of the traditional female role, as women have become more able to develop economic independence. She argues that it

has encouraged increased sexual opportunism in the female sector of the population. This has led to a culture of condoned irresponsible behaviour among them, which affects children in negative ways.

IS COMPETITIVENESS IN GIRLS DISCOURAGED AS IT IS SEEN AS A 'TURN-OFF' FOR BOYS?

Walby may also be criticised for not taking account of other forms of social inequality, such as ethnicity and class as well as other cultural variations and the diversity of experiences among women.

SOCIAL CLASS AND ECONOMIC CHANGES

- Since 1996, the Equal Opportunities Commission has indicated that there has been a growth of about half a million jobs in the white-collar service industry (frequently filled by women). This could promote their social mobility.
- Two out of three women are in the labour market, nearly two thirds of them in full time work.
- At the same time there has been a steady loss of traditional 'male' jobs, especially in heavy manufacturing.
- These changes in patterns of work are accompanied by the need for talents which girls already appear to have from their successes in school. For example, those of good communication and language skills, cooperation, conscientious attitudes, sociability and flexibility.

Reid (1996) has argued from his analysis of various data that the evidence is clear that educational performance differs between social-class groups. He concludes that: 'changes in the inequalities of educational performance of the sexes is clear proof that both cultural setting and most aspects of the educational and social systems play a part in the determination of educational performance.'

He rejects the idea that intelligence (or IQ) is the explanation of different educational achievement between them. Class differences are the key factor. Children from professional homes have much greater chances of obtaining similar qualifications than those from lower-working class homes, irrespective of gender. It is his conclusion that any disadvantaged group needs to have resources targeted at them, by way of positive discrimination.

Ridell (1992) showed how attitudes towards the education of girls varied between classes; there was strong support for traditional roles among working-class men, whereas among mothers in both classes there was support for improved changes in the opportunities for females.

Saunders (1996) disputes the idea that parental class influences the outcome of a child's occupational career. He suggests that there is evidence to show that it is ability test scores of children at 11 which correlate more strongly with the class position they achieve at 22 than any other.

Abbott and Wallace (1997) point out that feminist critics have argued that stratification theory should be more concerned with gender inequalities. This should begin with a revision of the ways that class is derived from the occupational position of the male, who is invariably assumed to be 'the head of the household.' This is a sexist classification which ignores the fact that women have their own subjective class identification which is not predictive from the husband or partner's occupation. When a woman marries there is no reason for her to take on her husband's educational status. They conclude that women's class placement should be determined by their own occupations and self-assessments.

Points of evaluation
1 It could be argued that the economic position of women is less related to eductional attainment than that of males. **Abbott** has cast doubt on the thesis that women are becoming more upwardly mobile. They still tend to fill less prestigious occupations, despite improved academic success. This is supported by **Crompton and Sanderson** (1986) who argue that sex-typing of jobs as female has resulted in their losing status and economic reward. Government policies between 1970–84 introduced an equality package intended to improve the rights of women; but there is evidence that they have not been fully successful in achieving equal pay (for broadly equal work) by the year 2000.

2 The views of Saunders are criticised by opponents because IQ tests are seen as weak instruments and even contemporary SATs subject to unreliable marking schemes.

3 Postmodernists argue that the debate about social class and its impact is no longer relevant because the distinctions used have become invalid. Classes have given way to consumer groups, who create their identity on the basis of the ways they purchase goods, select programmes to watch, make leisure choices and become subject to the impact of global markets. If women are improving their educational status it is in terms of choices about lifestyles.

4 Radical feminists argue that the only way to effect significant changes in gender relations is through class struggle and the politicisation of women.

BIOLOGY AND MOTIVATION

Biological theories are favoured by the New Right. They are used to account for differences in attainment between males and females in school on the grounds that physiological factors (including differences in hormones, chromosomes, brain and body structure) all result in natural and inevitable inequalities. Among innate differences sometimes identified are the views that girls have advantages in school over boys because they work harder and are better motivated; are more conscientious; have better levels of concentration; are better organised and mature earlier.

Points of evaluation
Biological explanations are opposed most strongly by radical feminists who see patterns of social behaviour arising from the economic structure of society. They argue that such theories are misguided because:

• They ignore sociological evidence which explains such behaviour in relation to social ideologies, norms and patterns of socialisation.
• They imply that behaviour is determined and outcomes inevitable.

On the other hand the radical feminists are sometimes criticised for failing to acknowledge the progress that girls have made in comparison with that of boys. They are said to assume an economic form of determinism.

Hakim (1996) has said: 'we must stop presenting women as victims or as an undifferentiated mass of mindless zombies whose every move is determined by other actors and social forces.'

FACTORS WITHIN THE SCHOOL

There are many interrelated factors to explain the differential levels of achievement of boys and girls. Apart from those factors external to the school, there are also issues within the institution which must be considered. These include:

1 The curriculum; school hierarchy and its organisation
2 Peer group cultures
3 Teacher expectations; labelling theory.

THE CURRICULUM

Feminists argue that one of the reasons why girls were found to be weaker than boys in some subjects, especially science and technology, before 1980, was the result of differential attitudes of teachers who had assumed girls had less ability. Boys were favoured in the classroom and intimidated girls in these lessons. In the 1990s there was evidence that the attitudes of girls were changing as they began to assess their choice of GCSE and A level subjects to career orientations and work opportunities. They were increasingly less passive in the processes of socialisation and education.

Once the concern for the underachievement of girls was recognised, policies were devised to remedy the problem and have been influential in directing girls into areas which they may otherwise avoid. New initiatives included:

• Women into Science and Engineering (WISE)
• Girls and Technology Education (GATE)
• Girls into Science and Technology (GIST)
• Experiments in single sex classes
• Revisions to GCSE and A level examinations: modules and coursework, the introduction of which may have enabled the conscientious girls to perform even better, although the exam marking schemes offer limited gains from these areas.

Sharpe (1994) has said through school organisation, and the curriculum (both overt and hidden) girls are still taught skills suitable for women's work, in which they will encounter some measure of discrimination.

Points of evaluation
Liberal feminists have argued that because of their work in sensitising people to such problems there is evidence that girls are beginning to outperform boys in some areas. More radical feminists are less sure that the patriarchal structures within the education system, together with entrenched teacher attitudes, can be defeated. They advocate more radical changes to assist women in the future.

Some critics of the attempts to make science subjects more appealing to girls have argued that this may have the effect of undermining their success levels in arts subjects and push them into greater competition with boys who inevitably will still continue to fill the highest occupational positions. *DES Report* 1992 said that in most institutions the gap between policy (for equality) and practice was still unacceptably wide. It is apparent from the statistics (see Tables 15, 16, 17) that despite the various initiatives gender differences remain in subject options.

PEER GROUP PRESSURE

The ideologies relating to the impact of patriarchal values on women have been the main focus of attention among feminist writers, and **Skeggs** (1995) has examined the ways in which the values of masculinity are established and sustained. Male groups (often with male teacher collusion) encourage an attitude of male power and dominance. They locate 'out groups' to ridicule and have means of dealing with boys who do not conform to the values of the 'in group', often in overtly brutal ways, but also in subtle ways which deride and embarrass. The outcome is that boys need to dominate girls and non-conforming boys to demonstrate the powers of their own masculinity. Girls lose confidence in science lessons, where boys dominate.

Spender (1983) noted from her research how males dominate conversation and discussion in classrooms. Those without power take more submissive roles. Girls learn this attitude in the classroom and discover that by avoiding a dominant role they become less of a threat and more acceptable to their peers. Girls informed her that it was natural for boys to ask questions and take more aggressive roles. They were more inclined to blame themselves for any failures and saw success as due to luck; boys took an opposite view.

TEACHER EXPECTATIONS: LABELLING THEORY

Interactionists point out how girls are marginalised in classrooms; boys continue to receive more attention from teachers, even though girls are achieving better results. Teachers' responses to pupils can affect behaviour and academic progress. **Kelly** (1987) has noted a masculine bias in textbooks, with few references to women in achieving roles. They further note how pupils develop their self-identities in the classroom interactions. A boy's conception of his masculinity is developed in relation to his male and female peers.

The research prompted improvements in teacher training to make new teachers more aware of the dangers of gender stereotyping. However, they have not always been amenable to attempts to change attitudes. Many work with beliefs in the biological explanations for gender differences in attainment and subject choice or that family background makes any attempt to intervene on their part with advice a waste of time. The older generation may also retain values which sustain beliefs in the inevitability of inequality and their skill in spotting the bright from the dull, and the few who will 'make the grade'.

Points of evaluation
Some feminists have argued that many aspects of women's inferior position in modern society is a result of the impact the industrial revolution and the growth of capitalism. The fact that girls are showing improvements in attainment levels has not changed their economic position, where they are still less well paid than men and have fewer chances of reaching top positions. Functionalists point to the

statistics which show the increasing academic achievements of girls in keeping ahead of boys since the mid 1980s. They see the educational system to be functioning effectively for girls and it is the failing boys that require more consideration.

THE DECLINE IN BOYS' ATTAINMENTS

Cohen (1998) notes the increasing anxiety revealed in the mid 1990s about boys' underachievement. It is said by many educationists to be one of the most disturbing problems facing the education system. She shows that from a historical perspective, boys have always underachieved. In 1689, John Locke wrote about the widespread failure of boys to master Latin, despite spending years studying it. In 1921 the headmaster of Rugby was complaining that the written English of a large proportion of boys was 'clumsy and painful to the verge of illiteracy...it seemed to be regarded by masters and boys as a natural defect.' In the eighteenth century, authors wrote of 'the inferiority of the female mind' and 'because boys were thoughtful and deep, they appeared slow and dull.'

But this fact has never been treated as a problem because male achievements have always been treated as symptomatic of something from within (their intellect). Their underachievements have been seen as something external (the way the school system is organised; or unsatisfactory teaching methods). For girls, the analysis has been the reverse. The overachieving girl was an abnormality whereas the underachieving boy was seen, even in recent times, as an expression of typical boyish ('laddish') behaviour. It even became an index of mental health, according to a Board of Education pronouncement in 1923. Boys were safe from overuse of mental energy because of their habit of 'healthy idleness'. Girls were more at risk because of their industrious and conscientious approach. In a book about language teaching in 1930, the author wrote 'many girls will work at a subject they dislike. No healthy boy ever does.' This taken-for-granted view meant no further theorising was required.

Cohen concludes that the question is not 'why are boys underachieving', but 'why boys' underachievement has now become an object of concern?' Her answer is that it is not just the result of the destruction of the industrial base of Britain; nor is it the result of pressure put on men by feminism, or by girls' superior achievement in recent years. It is because the discussions about achievement, academic success and attainment all have boys as their main object. But the call for a new focus on boys is not new, but merely perpetuates the historical process which has always assumed boys to have special potential which has not been fully developed. Their under achievement has been protected from scrutiny. She suggests that the first step is to problematise boys not girls and the construction of masculinity, which occurs in the home and among peers.

THE WIDER SOCIAL CONTEXT

Mahony (1999) notes that the preoccupation with boys' academic achievements is not confined to the UK. Debates have also been in progress in Australia, Canada, New Zealand and the USA, as well as Denmark, Germany and Japan. She argues that the issues must be considered in the context of the global economy. The DfEE said in 1997 that the global economy presents new opportunities and risks, where goods, services, capital and information are highly mobile and success depends more and more on the skills of the workforce. The debate about the achievement levels of boys and ways in which capitalist economics is operating worldwide affects the expectations about the role that men should play in it.

ISSUES OF MASCULINITY

Jackson (1999) suggests that although the crisis of men and masculinity is not new (it is a problem rediscovered by every generation), it re-emerged in the 1980s for several reasons. It became associated with the growth of feminism, the gay movement, AIDS, the decline of Britain as a major power, growing unemployment, and the need for a more flexible and better qualified work force.

The concern shown by educationists to remedy male underachievement led some feminists to interpret the moves as part of an anti-feminist backlash deflecting attention from the interests of girls. They feared that this may eventually lead to a restoration of traditional gender relations and male power in family, school and work. **Jackson** said that: 'already, for some white working class boys in humiliating economic and social circumstances there has been an attempt to forge a new meaning to their lives by reasserting manly, English pride through violent racism and xenophobia.

With traditional gender roles and power structures undermined, changing economic needs and regular publication of statistical data, the revelation that some boys have always performed poorly in secondary education has become more apparent. He opposes the idea of confrontational models, of girls' disadvantages versus boys' disadvantages, because they hinder the opportunity of a more open dialogue with people working together to produce a genuine equality of opportunity within schools and in wider society.

In his analysis, he describes how feminists have pointed to the facts that:

- Teachers, parents and others in authority have traditionally viewed boys' bad behaviour as 'natural' and turned a blind eye to it.
- There has been an invisibility of boys as gendered beings. Their masculinities have been part of a taken-for-granted norm: white heterosexual man equals a human being.
- The 'boys will be boys' assumption needs to be challenged.

He suggests that in this respect feminists have produced a valuable reminder that in reality conventional manliness is a construction, that can change. However, although they can be identified, there are major problems in tackling the underachieving boys. It has been argued that macho stereotypes are preventing suicidal young men from asking for help; in 1999 12 men aged 15–24 were killing themselves each week. They may also be more violent in their personal relationships.

THE SIGNIFICANCE OF PEER CULTURE

Jackson has pointed out how many of the failing working-class boys are tied deeply into a traditional macho boys culture where academic work is feminised, associated with feminine qualities. There is a strong relationship between their failure in school, their alienation and powerlessness, macho values and their perceived limited work opportunities. They therefore turn to compensatory sources of status. This is located in their notions of dominant heterosexual masculinity.

POLICY ISSUES

Jackson says that educationists are faced with the problem of changing school cultures where underachievement is a valued norm and where success in school is not seen as a normal masculine activity. Schools would need to investigate and challenge areas of bullying in which boys gain power over girls (and some boys) by sexual harassment; the ways they tease, insult and use sexist jokes to intimidate girls; they need to expose how the factors in wider society (especially the mass media, computer games, the economics of large-scale sports enterprises) influence these male values.

However, he argues that it is important to remember that boys are not 'the real victims' of changing forces in society at the end of the twentieth century. Many girls are still subject to the infamous glass ceiling. Although improving qualification levels, they also require encouragement, confidence and opportunities to increase their chances of success and good career opportunities. He advocates viewing schools: 'as complex arenas of power, where both masculine and feminine identities are actively made each day, through dynamic processes of negotiation, refusal and struggle.'

Activity
'With more women and men working together, there will be more opportunities for changing gender inequalities' or will men ensure that they retain even more control?

THE SIGNIFICANCE OF THE HOME

Murphy and Elwood (1999) argue that young children learn gender preferences, in terms of interests and pastimes, in the home and with peers. It arises from the ways that parents treat their children and the expectations they have of them. This leads them to pursue particular interests which provide different learning opportunities and align them in different ways to schooling and to subject learning. The interests and skills learnt in the home combine with the ways teachers perceive and treat them in school. This leads to differentials in performance which may be quite unrelated to ability. They also lead to underachievement as many children channel themselves away from certain learning experiences. For example, surveys in the UK and USA showed that girls' and boys' experience of scientific equipment and apparatus out of school differed.

- Boys had greater access to it in the home through equipment provided by parents. Ultimate performance differences increased in range and magnitude as students progressed through school.
- Boys played more with electrical toys and gadgets outside school, which familiarised them with the effects of electricity and to develop an understanding of how it can be controlled. This assisted them in subsequent science lessons.

In the same way, performance in English was also related to interests outside school. Girls were more likely to:

- Read stories, than comics or books about hobbies, (preferred by boys)
- Read to help them understand their own and other people's problems
- Develop their writing skills

All of this assisted them in developing abilities of value in examinations requiring language skills. Such research data led the government in 1999 to launch a national initiative to improve standards of literacy and numeracy with all people, both children and adult learners.

INSIDE SCHOOL FACTORS

Barber (1994) suggests that boys' disaffection with school in comparison to girls, is related particularly to their motivation to learn.

- Girls were consistently more positive, better motivated, developed better relationships with teachers and were generally better behaved than boys in their mid-teens.
- Teacher–pupil interactions were identified as being very significant. For girls, feedback from teachers focused more on their work rather than their behaviour;

for boys the reverse was true. The low expectations of girls in science reinforced their own self-images; boys frequently overestimated their abilities.

- Negative teacher labelling for some boys undermined their confidence and interest in school. For both boys and girls, where motivation in a subject is low, achievement tends to be low.

Reed (1999) points out the close links between 'under-achieving boys' and 'failing schools', according to Ofsted definitions. In 1997, of 402 failing schools, 70 were special schools with high proportions of boys on roll. The characteristic features of the failing school include many closely associated with the wider underachievement of boys: 'standards of literacy...are too low...behaviour seriously affects learning...attendance is unsatisfactory and puntuality often poor; exclusion rates are high and for boys from ethnic minorities very high...there are more boys than girls in the schools that are not providing acceptable standards of education.'

Hey et al (1999) undertook research to evaluate why Special Educational Needs provision was dominated by males. It is forthcoming where a child has difficulties which cannot be met from the usual resources provided by a school. These needs are identified by an educational psychologist, according to strict criteria. The authors noted different learning styles were reported. Boys were less keen to seek help from their male peers and if it wasn't forthcoming from teachers; they went off-line and responded with disruptive behaviour. They argue that schools must organise their practices in ways that work against the common-sense views that 'boys will be boys'.

Epstein et al (1999) state that levels of attainment in traditional male and female subjects are reversed as students move from GCSE to A level. Statistically, the small number of girls who take A level physics are likely to do better than the boys; in English and languages, boys who take them at A level do better than girls. As they move on to university, the gendered effect is that men tend to get more first-class degrees than women. Overall, the underachievement of boys in school is strongly related to class and ethnicity.

The authors of **Failing Boys** argue that it is the conclusion of many researchers that not all boys are failing in school; the statistics may mask the fact that it is some boys (as well as some girls) who fail, especially at the secondary level.

- They reject the idea that any one theory explains a complex issue.
- They look to ideas for intervening in schooling which will improve the education of both boys and girls.
- They also advocate the introduction of progressive policies and practices and a greater awareness among teachers of key issues arising from the moral panic around boys' 'underachievement.' which should not be seen as just the responsibility of schools.

SUMMARY

Since the 1970s girls have improved their academic results whilst boys have failed to improve theirs. But at post-secondary and in higher education they regain their advantages. This is also true in the work place, where femals remain under-represented in top positions. In secondary education girls are thought to do well for several reasons, associated with the ways they are socialised in the home and among their peers. Whilst the family and work structures have changed in radical ways in the latter part of the twentieth century, the male role may have been more negatively affected than the female. Feminists claim they have raised awareness among girls and teachers about the need to encourage positive attitudes among them; many refute the idea that there should be more attention paid on the under-achievement of boys in secondary schools, which for some commentators is a long-standing historical issue. One of the policy issues is for improved teacher training to ensure that new teachers are well aware of the problem areas within a gendered society and of the complexity of the issues.

STUDY GUIDE

Exam Tips

1 Write for marks. Each part of an exam question has a specified number of them. Produce many facts or pieces of evidence rather than one detailed point.
2 Exam questions test what you know. Do not attempt a question for which you have not prepared.
3 Read the instructions in the question carefully. You may be asked to evaluate; discuss; explain; critically examine. Be sure that you respond accordingly.

Exam Hints

1 The role of the teacher as an agent of social control is important in assessing the role of the hidden curriculum in maintaining gender inequality. Discuss.
2 The improved performances of girls in the educational system has not been matched by boys. How can this be explained?
3 Explain and evaluate the contributions of feminist theorists to an understanding of either female educational improvement or male failures in recent years.

9

ETHNICITY AND EDUCATION

Introduction

THIS CHAPTER EXAMINES the explanations for differentials in the educational performance of members of ethnic minority groups. The factors presented in research look at cultural differences and possible aspects of deprivation as well as economic issues of class and social causes of racism. The concerns inside the school have been in terms of attitudes of teachers and peers, as well as the perceptions of pupils themselves. There are areas of unresolved controversy, especially in relation to the interpretation of data and whether the purpose is to reveal knowledge using the most scientific methods possible, or to use findings, often from observational studies, to argue for changes to overcome injustices within the educational and wider social system.

Table 16: *Key Authors, Concepts and Issues in this Chapter*		
KEY AUTHORS	KEY CONCEPTS	KEY ISSUES
Swann	Biological racism	IQ discounted as a factor in explaining ethnic underachievement
Rutter	School environment	Impact on attainment levels
Clarke	Underachievement	Insufficient studies directed at use of language
Kysel Modood and Shiner	Ethnic background	Some minority groups perform better than white peers Some are over-represented in university applications

Jones	Parental qualification	Impact on child's attainment
Abbot and Wallace	Female career aspirations	These vary between minority groups and are related to class
Bordieu	Cultural capital	This is an additional problem for minority groups members
Reid	Class and ethnicity	This combination influences underachievement
Mabey and Mackay	Educational disadvantages	This is seen in the most vulnerable members of minority groups
Whitmarsh and Summerfield	Social disadvantage	The impact on ethnic minorities
Mirza	Radical strategies	Afro-Caribbean females have high educational aspirations
Drew and Demack	Statistical analysis	Data presents comparative analysis between white and black children
Daniel MacIntosh and Smith	Prejudice and discrimination	Evidence that it was endemic in society
Lewis	New Right	Evidence for racism is overstated overstated
Wright	Stereotypes	Evidence that primary school teachers have negative expectations
Gillborn	Racist myths	Evidence that they occur more strongly in secondary schools
Foster, Gomm and Hammersley	Victimised teachers	Argues that teachers are not to blame for underachieving minorities
Bhatti Fleming	Pupil perceptions	Evidence that pupils do see racism in teachers
Hall	Social memory	There is selective exclusion of black history from schools
Jaggi	Selective amnesia	Also from local communities
Connolly	Community attitudes	These affect attitudes of children and teachers' perceptions

Smith and Tomlinson	Racial tolerance	Found a lack of racial antagonism
Jackson	Effeminised learning	Some black children oppose school culture through macho values
Sewell	Peer groups	Five categories identified

IDEOLOGY, RACE, ETHNICITY AND EDUCATION

There is no universally accepted meaning of the word 'race'. Sociologists emphasise the way that beliefs about the world are socially constructed and how concepts of superiority and inferiority emerge in a status society in relation to competition for power, prestige and scarce economic resources. Racist ideologies are used to justify the oppression of some (defined as inferior foreigners or immigrants) by others. Technically, an immigrant is anyone who has *recently* arrived from another society in which they have habitually lived; of black people in Britain over 40 per cent are British born. Racism (the belief and practice of discrimination and prejudice) is based on the misinformed notion that people can be racially categorised. Ethnic groups describe those who share cultural characteristics (food, language, dress, religion) and often a skin colour, which are different from those of the indigenous population. From the differences in lifestyle and life chances, stereotypes emerge which have a deleterious effect on those subjected to them.

BLACK MINORITIES AND EDUCATIONAL ATTAINMENT

Until the 1980s little statistical data was collected in relation to minority groups. The 1991 census was the first to ask questions about ethnic origin. However, that which is now available show a pattern of educational levels of achievement among black ethnic minority groups, which for some has not changed significantly, and which for others shows improvements and in some cases success levels above those of the indigenous white population.

Table 17: *Educational attainments of ethnic groups in five English LEAs 1981–2*			
QUALIFICATIONS	ASIAN	AFRO-CARIBBEAN	OTHERS
1 A level or more	13	5	13
5 higher grade GCE O/CSE +	17	19	19
No graded results	19	19	19

Source: Swann Report. 1985

Table 18: *Participation rates of 16 and 19 years olds in full-time education by age and ethnic group*		
	AGE 16	AGE 19
White	75	21
Afro-Caribbean	79	32
Indian	89	50
Pakistani	84	40
Bangladeshi	77	22
Chinese	97	74

Source: Drew et al 1997

Asian children were performing as well as their white peers, while Afro-Caribbeans were doing less well.

The participation rates for all minority groups were higher than for whites, suggesting a strong belief in the value of educational qualifications. Apart from Pakistani and Bangladeshi groups, there were more females staying on in school.

Policy Studies Institute Report 1997 showed:

• Ethnic minorities are increasingly more likely to continue their education beyond the age of 16 than white pupils.
• Apart from Caribbean men and Bangladeshi women, they are more likely to apply for university places.
• Young Caribbean men have fewer educational qualifications than other groups.

Explanations have been put forward to account for the variations and the changes over time.

Explanations to account for variations in attainments among minority groups
1   **Biological factors** (non sociological)
2   **Cultural Difference Theory**
    The focus of attention is on issues relating to differences in use of language, religion, dress and aspirations.
3   **Cultural Deprivation Theory**
    The focus of attention is on issues relating the home background. The possible lack of cultural capital, poverty, and unemployment.
4   **Socio-economic factors**
    The focus is on class factors and issues of ethnicity and racism.

5 **Institutional factors**
   Attention is paid to what happens in school; teacher expectations and perceptions, the relevance of the curriculum and peer pressures.

However, the issues are sensitive and complex and there is a danger in generalising ethnic minority cultures so that they provide stereotypical implications. Cultural patterns are related to class and status, and variations are just as subtle as in those relating to members of households containing non-black people. Children from minority backgrounds perform at different attainment levels; some very successfully, others less so.

BIOLOGICAL EXPLANATIONS

Biological racism is the belief in the hereditary inferiority of black races. The idea that differences in intelligence are due to innate factors, based on studies which have claimed that whites perform better on intelligence tests, have been completely discounted. The test procedures have been subject to critical attack. The **Swann Committee** (1985) produced a major report based on detailed research and discounted the significance of IQ as a factor in explaining differentials in attainment between white and various black minority groups (some of whom outperformed white children in examinations).

EVIDENCE FOR CULTURAL DIFFERENCES

The values of the home and peers have been examined over time to see how far cultural factors are influential in affecting educational outcomes. The conclusions from studies between 1970–99 are that they appear to be significant influences. Although there are few which carefully examine the effects of religious beliefs, some have noted the possible significance of language development.

Rutter et al (1974) found from their research in London and the Isle of Wight (IOW) evidence to show the significance of the school environment to account for differences in attainment. Those from the poorer parts of London, with impoverished early years and subject to prejudice and discrimination were at an educational disadvantage. The parental class, and educational background was similar for both groups. They found:

(i) Non-immigrant London 10 year olds showed more difficulties than their counterparts of the IOW in relation to reading, emotional problems and conduct disorders.

(ii) On tests of reading ability the West Indian children produced a mean score 13 months below that of children from non-immigrant families.

(iii) Within the West Indian group attainment differed markedly according to the child's place of birth. Those born in the UK had a reading age 10 months above their counterparts born in the West Indies. Both groups had similar class backgrounds.

Clarke (1997) makes the point that there have been insufficient studies directed at the issues of language and as a result the findings are complex and must interrelate with other factors. She suggests that it may be in some cases those arriving in Britain from parts of Asia had greater access to the English language than others. The Bangladeshis' rural background provides more limited chances in this respect. Those from various parts of India, Pakistan and Bangladesh may speak as many as eight different languages.

Kysel (1988) showed that both Indian and Pakistani pupils performed better than white working-class pupils, whereas Bangladeshi children were underachieving.

Modood and Shiner (1994) noted that Indian and Pakistani students were over-represented in applications for Higher Education. Again, Bangladeshi students were under-represented.

SIGNIFICANCE OF RELIGION

For some minority groups, religious values may be a source of encouragement to increase qualifications and achievement.

(a) For Sikhs religious values are a significant part of day-to-day life. There were about 400,000 in Britain in 2000. They emphasise the acquisition of skills and successful educational performance to enhance status and individual responsibility.

(b) The Jewish groups in Britain have been a highly successful sector in many areas of social life, influenced by the Rabinic tradition which has always emphasised the need for excellence in work and study.

(c) There are about 500,000 Afro-Caribbeans in Britain; the effects of alienation, prejudice and racism increased the interest of some from this background in religious movements, as a source of support and community. For some teachers, the attachment to Rastafarianism by younger West Indians may have been a source of friction and misunderstanding.

(d) Hinduism involves a belief in reincarnation, a moral law and mystical contemplation. It supports a caste system, and traditionally, those in the most prestigious castes achieve the highest standards of education. It advocates ideals of obedience.

(e) Muslims form the largest non-Christian minority in Britain, with about a million members of the Islamic community in 2000. The younger generation, like others in contemporary Britain, is less religious than the older. The beliefs of Islam promote the rights of women, stressing their equality, their rights to study, work and to take an active part in society.

SIGNIFICANCE OF DRESS

The ways in which people dress are related to their cultural background; cultural values are also class related and become the subject of stereotypical images. The working class may once have been associated with the 'cloth cap'; the middle-class professional with a bowler hat and the public school teacher with a mortar board.

Study point
For those in ethnic minority groups who are closely attached to specific cultural mores, the clothes they wear may serve to 'confirm' to teachers both positive and negative images. Suggest examples, and show how the stereotypes operate.

The failure of teachers and peers to appreciate the cultural significance of dress may lead to racist responses.

PARENTAL ASPIRATIONS

Many studies have indicated that the parents of children in black minority groups are generally very encouraging. Muslim girls appear to be more subject to limited career aspirations in Britain.

Rutter et al (1974) found that the parents did as much as they could to assist their children with school work and showed great concern about them, but because of low incomes were forced to work long and often unsociable hours, giving them less time to spend interacting with their children.

Jones (1993) illustrated how the educational background of parents affected the standards of their children. In both black and white families, children whose parents had no qualifications performed significantly worse than those who did have them, on tests of attainment. Whereas about 75 per cent of Bangladeshi parents had no qualifications, only 12 per cent of children from this group took A levels or beyond. This contrasted with 31 per cent who did so whose parents came from India. Social Trends (1997–98) showed that in 1997–98 15 per cent of men and 20 per cent of women from white groups in G.B. held no formal qualification compared with 22 per cent of men and 33 per cent of women from India and Pakistan and Bangladesh; although men from these groups were more likely to have a degree than the white men.

Abbott and Wallace (1997) indicate that it still seems to be the case that middle class and Afro-Caribbean girls have career aspirations in terms of secure employment and marriage, as do Chinese and non-Muslim Asian girls, whereas Muslim Asian women tend to withdraw from the labour market permanently on marriage. Researchers at Sheffield Hallam University reported in 1999 that many women from this sector are forcibly confined to the home for long periods; breaking free from these constraints can be exceptionally difficult, especially if they have children. They are affected by immigration status, lack of language skills and absence of extrafamilial support networks. It is interesting to note that in Saudi Arabia, an Islamic society, the number of female graduates (87,000) outstripped the number of males (79,000) in 1998. There the stated government belief is that no one is permitted to undermine or marginalise the active role of women in society.

Points of evaluation

1   Cultural Difference Theory places emphasis on the social and economic differences which exist between the culture of the home background from which the minority members come and that of the school which they attend.
2   Disadvantages arise for some, because they may lack the ability to use the language adequately or share the same goals.
3   Those who emphasise their own cultural differences may fare least well because the teachers may not be sympathetic or understanding; whereas some may become invisible, and not participate or interact with the teacher in positive ways in the classroom.

EVIDENCE FOR CULTURAL DEPRIVATION

CULTURAL CAPITAL DEFICITS

Bordieu describes the educational system as an agency for reproducing middle class values. Those who share these and whose children are imbued with them will succeed best within the system. Ethnic minority groups who lack the cultural capital at the outset may consequently have less opportunity to attain high success in later life.

Reid (1996) agrees that 'ethnic differences in achievement may well be due to class or class in combination with ethnicity'. Those members of the ethnic minority groups who do not achieve well are more likely to be members of the lower social classes, among whom white children are also least successful.

Mabey (1986) has also argued that class is the most significant factor in determining educational attainments; there is danger, therefore in focusing too much on ethnic origin at the expense of factors of economic stratification in a class society.

POVERTY

MacKay (1999) argues that whilst a historical perspective of education suggests that there has been a constant move towards greater justice and equity, yet in

1999 the most vulnerable members of society in terms of gender, race and disability were over-represented in the lowest socio-economic groups (see Table 22).

Data from *Office of Population Censuses and Surveys* (OPCS) 1991 and the **Equal Opportunities Commission** (EOC) 1996 showed that those groups over-represented in the poorest sectors of society included:

- Minority ethnic families
- Lone parent families (in nine out of ten of which the parent is a woman)
- Large families with young children and families with people with disabilities.

MacKay suggests that discrimination and injustice are endemic. If a large sector of society only has access to an impoverished quality of life, then significant issues of justice arise. Those who are poor (living significantly below average standards of living) suffer much worse life chances than those who are not. They may literally expect a shorter life span; have more serious illnesses; have worse access to medicine and enjoy a poorer level of education and all that follows in terms of occupational chances (see Table 19).

UNEMPLOYMENT

It is apparent that those with fewest educational qualifications fare least well in the occupational structure, having least choice. Black minority groups are also subject to prejudice and discrimination in the workplace, making upward career mobility more difficult.

Policy Studies Institute Report (1997) showed that:

- There is evidence that many black and Asian people are worse off than white people with similar qualifications; nor have their average earnings caught up with those of white workers although the gap has narrowed.
- Young Caribbean men have fewer educational qualifications than other groups. Most of the unqualified are among the long-term unemployed.

Table 19: % of those in different ethnic groups who are unemployed or suffering disability					
	AFRO-CARIBBEAN	INDIAN	PAKISTANI	BANGLADESHI	UK MEAN
Unemployed					
Less than 6 months	6	2	4	4	2
More than 6 months	17	11	13	18	5
Permanently sick	5	4	6	4	3

Source: Whitmash and Summerfield (*Social Focus on Ethnic Minorities*, 1996)

Points of evaluation

(i) There is a danger in assuming that cultural deficiency implies that working class or black cultures are inferior to those of the white (middle-class) sector of society, which is not the case.

(ii) **Mirza** (1997) found from her study of two inner city working-class schools that black girls did as well, if not better, than their peers in average exam performances. Many of them had high aspirations, and duly achieved them. She concludes that 'doing well can become a radical strategy.'

SOCIO-ECONOMIC FACTORS

CLASS

The different patterns of response to class position among different minority groups is problematic without detailed research. It appears that in some cases Asian groups have been particularly effective in developing their market situation. They have retained their sense of ethnicity through living in similar areas, working in similar jobs and have become effective cohesive groups within their communities. Many of those who first arrived in Britain were typically youngest sons of small land-owning families with good education and with strong religious values to guide their behaviour. The attempts to retain aspects of their traditional cultural values has led to the development of special Islamic schools in which language and culture can be taught.

There have consistently been a small proportion of Asian immigrants (especially with an Indian background) who are within middle class categories, such as those who came to Britain in the 1970s from East Africa. They have successfully maintained their traditions of business enterprise. In addition, they entered a wide range of professions, including law, teaching and medicine.

Those from a West Indian origin generally lacked this kind of background. They had a history of slavery and subservience which was portrayed in most American films until recent times, where a black person was invariably a servant. It may be hypothesised that such cultural background factors would affect opportunities for educational and subsequent occupational successes.

Those from Bangladesh and Afro-Caribbean countries tended to take occupational positions at the lower end of the socio-economic scale. They were encouraged to come by British politicians during the period 1952–65 to fill positions in unskilled and semi-skilled occupations as Britain recovered economically after the war. The need was for a mobile manual labour force. The high concentration of female nurses came from the West Indies; whereas there were few professional males arriving.

Cole (1999) refers to data adapted from Labour Force Surveys (1988, 89 and 90) to illustrate the class structure of Britain based on job levels and ethnicity.

Table 20: *Job levels according to ethnicity and gender (%)*

ETHNIC GROUP	OCCUPATIONAL CATEGORY							
	MALES				FEMALES			
	1	11	111	1V	1	11	111	1V
All origins	27	27	32	19	11	55	5	29
White	27	20	33	19	11	56	5	29
Afro-Caribbean	12	19	39	29	8	54	4	34
Indian	25	18	29	28	10	47	5	38
Pakistani	12	16	34	37	4	42	7	47
Bangladeshi	12	14	5	70	*	*	*	*
Chinese	30	19	10	40	16	53	2	29

Source: Labour Force Surveys (1988,89 and 90)

Activity

What does the information reveal with regard to:

- Class variations (within groups as well as between them; note the position of Chinese men)?
- The position of women?
- The structure of the ethnic lower working class (both men and women) in relation to the white population?

The extent to which class factors affect educational development may be seen in Table 22 The data was gathered from a Youth Cohort Study of England and Wales (a nationally representative study) in which gender differences and ethnic background and class position are analysed. The scores of exam entrants are analysed, using A=7–G=1. The data show that ethnic differences are significant; class differences appear greater.

Drew and Demack (1998) note that:

- Black middle-class pupils performed well at GCSE
- White working-class males perform poorly as do black Afro-Caribbean females
- Asian males and females performed most consistently in each class group.

Table 21: *Educational performance of GCSE candidates (points scored) in class groups from national Youth Cohort Study*			
	PROFESSIONAL	INTERMEDIATE	MANUAL
Afro-Caribbean female	25	18	16
Asian female	28	26	23
White female	32	26	21
Afro-Caribbean male	27	21	14
Asian male	31	27	23
White male	30	24	18

Source: Drew and Gray (1990)

RACISM

In 1999 the report following the inquiry into the murder of a black A level student, Stephen Lawrence, said that racism exists in every area of society, irrespective of the intentions of well-meaning administrators.

Daniel (1966) writing in 1968, said: 'Discrimination forces immigrants into self-supporting, separate groups in society; these have definable status, function and level of influence, i.e: the lowest status, the most menial function and the lowest level of influence; they begin to form a new social class, a new proletariat.'

Studies have been conducted from time to time since that date, but evidence remains of racist attitudes affecting educational attainment of the children within black ethnic minority groups.

The *Swann Report* (1985) stated that differentials in educational attainment were still related to socio-economic factors, including racism and poverty.

• West Indian children were not faring as well as Asians and white children (three times as many of whom achieved the highest grades at 16).
• The social and economic problems identified by **Rutter et al** (1974) remained significant obstacles.
• Teachers were blamed for failing to recognise differences in cultural attitudes and values as causes of differences in attainment.

In the recommendations, Swann opposed the idea that ethnic minorities should set up their own schools and the view that schools should adopt bilingual teaching. But the report did encourage the introduction of new policies to assist children from minority groups to combat racism; the learning of English and the promotion of the idea that Britain is a multiracial and multicultural society.

PREJUDICE AND DISCRIMINATION

Prejudice describes the process of prejudging a person or group (usually in negative ways) on the basis of cultural or physical characteristics. Discrimination is the act of prejudice. It has been unlawful since 1965 to treat a person less favourably on the grounds of colour, race or ethnic origin. Many studies have been conducted since the 1960s to monitor their presence. These include research by **Daniel** (1966); **McIntosh and Smith** (1975); **CRE** (1980); **PSI** (1984; 1997); **the Society for Black Lawyers** (1992); they all concluded that racist attitudes were endemic throughout society, helping to account for the underachievement of many black children in schools. In 1999 the African and Caribbean Evangelical Alliance Report stated that they were preparing plans for a network of new full-time Church primary schools to combat racism and the underachievement of black children. They have already successfully pioneered Saturday Schools to supplement the standard curriculum.

Points of evaluation
Lewis (1988) is a New Right critic of such findings. He argues that the problems associated with race have been overstated. Opposition to a multiracial society is not necessarily irrational; prejudice and discrimination are inevitable (and functional) and cannot be eradicated by legislation. Anti-racism is seen as an invention of the socialist Left. However, opponents stress that the purpose of research and subsequent policy making should be to highlight areas of inequality and challenge them. They are critical of the New Right for feeding the views that ethnic pluralism raises problems for social and political cohesion in modern Britain. For the critics the evidence of prejudice and discrimination is overwhelming and therefore its effects on children in school must be combated and neutralised, so that future generations will have greater equality.

INSTITUTIONAL FACTORS — WHAT HAPPENS WITHIN THE SCHOOL

TEACHER PERCEPTIONS AND EXPECTATIONS

The (CRE) *Commission for Racial Equality Report* (1985) found that black pupils were four times more likely to be suspended or excluded than white children. Insensitive teachers were blamed who did not appreciate cultural differences as a cause of the behaviour of which they disapproved. Rastafarian culture was a common source of teacher–pupil friction. These findings were confirmed by **Wright** (1992) who showed how even in primary schools teachers often assumed that Afro-Caribbean boys would be badly behaved.

Gillborn (1990) presented similar findings in secondary schools. In his study of City Road Comprehensive, an inner city school in the Midlands, he describes the teachers' tendency to perceive a threat to their authority in many routine dealings with Afro-Caribbean students. This myth became an accepted (though largely unspoken) part of teachers' craft knowledge, their idea of how things really are. When they acted on their perceptions they increased the potential for further conflict. The response of the students was to develop more strongly their sense of ethnicity, their identity as young black people. This was in turn interpreted as a sign of aggression or 'the wrong attitude' by the teacher.

Wright (1988) provides evidence of many racist comments (some said 'jokingly') which were made about her by teachers in the staff-room, in the course of her classroom observation research. One is quoted as saying 'Hey what's this?' (pointing to her hair) 'All you need now is a bone through your nose and lip and you'd look like a real Zulu Queen.'

Points of evaluation

Some research supports the view that the school, especially teacher perceptions and attitudes can affect the performance of minority groups in negative (as well as positive ways). The work of **Gillborn et al** is particularly critical in this regard. **Wright's** experiences add weight to their views. However, other sociologists discount these factors and indicate that there are others which are more significant in determining low (and high) success levels among some minority groups.

- **Foster, Gomm and Hammersley** (1996) claim that there is no good reason to believe minority students are unfairly disadvantaged by school-based processes and especially by the actions of teachers.
- **Mirza** (1997) suggests that the gender issues need to be taken into account. Whilst West Indian boys may not be as successful as others, there is evidence that young Afro-Caribbean girls are expressing a desire and motivation to succeed within the educational system in the 1990s. This is described as a radical development which is both strategic and subversive.
- *The Policy Studies Institute Report* on ethnic minorities (1997) showed that members of all black ethnic minority groups were more likely to continue their education beyond 16 than their white peers. Apart from Caribbean men and Bangladeshi women members of other black ethnic minority groups were also more likely to seek entrance to university.

On the other hand, evidence from statistical data supports the fact that exclusion rates are high especially among Afro-Caribbeans.

- In 1992, 8 per cent of exclusions were within this category, even though they only formed 2 per cent of the school population.
- In 1997–8 the number of permanent exclusions fell; the decrease was larger among white than black boys; the proportion of black boys who were expelled rose.
- In 1996–7 Afro-Caribbean pupils were 4.2 times more likely than white pupils to be expelled and by 1997–8 they were 4.5 times more likely.

The **Commission for Racial Equality** states that these increases result from the failure of the government to target the racial element within schools.

PUPIL PERCEPTIONS

The *Black Child Report* (1997), based on interviews with 374 children of African and Afro-Caribbean descent aged between 11–16 years at schools in six major cities in Britain, showed levels of racism experienced by them.

Table 22: *% of sample experiencing racism*

EXAMPLES OF ISSUES RAISED AMONG BOYS AND GIRLS IN THE SAMPLE	RESPONSE
Have experienced racism by a teacher in the previous month	22%
Have experienced racism by other pupils in the previous month	15%
Would prefer to attend a black-only school	38%

Source: Black Class report (1997)

Bhatti (1999) also indicated that pupils did perceive their teachers as holding negative stereotypes about them, so that they had to learn special strategies to cope with the day to day problems. For example, they would keep quiet and nod many times in the teacher's presence, but have a decent laugh, smoke and unwind, with Asian peers out of school. They further developed a trendier image for the wider community. Asian girls developed two images; a goody-goody pose for teachers and a trendier one to test what was possible in the wider community. They identified good and bad teachers.

Fleming (1993) also reports many examples of personal acts of racism experienced by the pupils he interviewed, who vividly describe the abuse they received in the course of playing games.

Points of evaluation
Critics of the pupil perception responses argue that in their work they found that when pressed, pupils had difficulty in specifying what they meant by prejudice or racism, on the part of teachers and other peers. Others have noted that the samples from which information is derived are small and may not be representative. However, **Gillborn** has argued that the views of the pupils must be considered more carefully, since what they report is how they see the world and how they respond. Their views should not be disregarded or seen merely as a sign of pupil 'hostility'; rather, they should encourage a more analytical look at teacher–pupil interactions.

CURRICULUM CONTENT

There have been concerns expressed that for the three million black people in Britain, there has been little attempt to use the educational curriculum to provide insights into the cultural values of minorities. Nor are the historical factors which have influenced their positions in contemporary Britain examined. However, some attempts have been made to remedy these failings.

Hall (1999) called for 'a radical transformation of social memory' to better reflect 'the black British presence and the explosion of cultural diversity and difference which is everywhere our daily reality.'

Jaggi (1999) argues that Britain's mythology has been of a white core culture linked to an unbroken national tradition of white supremacy. This was fed by 500 years of conquest and colonisation. Some of those subsequently given national freedom, but who remained British passport holders, came to Britain in the 1950s to work. 'Yet a selective amnesia purges foreign elements from memory... writing them out of the country's idea of itself.' It is for such reasons that the **Commission for Racial Equality** (CRE) advised the government to include in the curriculum (for September 2000) a multicultural component in personal and social education, and a new programme of citizenship.

RACISM AND IDENTITY

Identities are constructed in the processes of day-to-day life inside and outside the school. They are shaped by the way teachers view and treat children as well as how they relate to their peers. The meaning of a racial identity is a particularly complex concept, it is not a coherent unity. A person's self-identity depends on context and changing circumstances. Yet, assumptions are made that for black children their identity is fixed in terms of colour and race.

Connolly (1998) showed that the attitudes of children and teachers were strongly influenced by the community attitudes and values of the area in which the school was set. Those seen as Indian, Pakistani or Bangladeshi were frequently viewed by whites as culturally exclusive. Older black Afro-Caribbean children were often seen as potentially disaffected and disruptive; Asian children were described in more positive ways; they were believed to have more supportive home backgrounds, the girls in particular being highly valued in the classroom, as quiet and diligent pupils. It is his argument that even in junior schools children and teachers are reworking and reproducing racialised ways of constructing identities.

Institutional racism:
There is debate as to whether schools are racist in terms of curriculum, streams, sets and ethos. Also, whether unconscious racist attitudes of teachers and other pupils account for the problems faced by black children. There are some sociologists who represent this view in their findings.

Wright (1987) argued that there are discriminatory practices in place in schools which result in differential treatment of children on the basis of their race or ethnicity, so that placement in sets and streams is not entirely a matter of ability. Afro-Caribbeans are particularly disadvantaged.

Gillborn (1999) made use of a range of methods to focus on the interactions between white teachers and minority group students, especially in relation to discipline and academic selection. He describes how racism operates as a complex and multifaceted aspect of school life and noted:

• How teacher expectations can lead to inequitable treatment.
• The irony that whilst the majority of teachers were clearly concerned with issues of equality, they invariably generalised, seeing conflict with Afro-Caribbean students as indicative of a more deep seated rejection of authority, typical of them as a group.
• The deep and subtle ways in which racism is institutionalised and effective in limiting the educational opportunities of black pupils.

Points of evaluation
Foster, et al (1996) have argued that from their critique of all the main research on racism in schools, the data used has not proved conclusively that racism exists 'beyond reasonable doubt'. They refer to the 'bogus scientific claims of researchers in this field'. In his book *Policy and Practice* (1990), **Foster** concludes that 'ethnic minority students enjoyed equal opportunities with their white peers.'

Smith and Tomlinson (1989) also noted racial tolerance and lack of antagonism in the schools they looked at, drawing attention to the contrast with previous work on racial harassment. **Ofsted** (1993–4) showed that exclusion for Indian, Bangladeshi and Chinese pupils is lower than that for white children, per thousand people.

However, **Gillborn** (1998) is critical of such findings arguing that when the account of Foster is scrutinised, there is a failure to:

• Define the concept of racism adequately
• Explain the fact that Afro-Caribbean males were over-represented in low teaching sets
• Present any critique of the ways in which the negative labels are attached to some black pupils.

In many respects the debate between **Foster** and **Gillborn** hinges on differences in research methodologies and in ideological positions regarding the aims of research studies. The former take the more traditionally conservative view that the aim of research into matters of race should be to produce knowledge relevant to public debates, not to eradicate inequality. **Gillborn** by contrast stresses the more radical position, of wishing to reveal problem areas to encourage changes in attitudes and to promote the introduction of policies which will remedy injustices and overcome inequalities.

Study point
Which of these two positions do you favour?

PEER INFLUENCES

Peer pressures are powerful forces in gaining the conformity of people in groups. See also Chapter 8.

Jackson (1998) notes how in the macho cultures of some Afro-Caribbean boys have been shown to exemplify a complex combination of compulsory heterosexuality, homophobia and misogyny.

Sewell (1999) suggests that this shared culture of cool indifference to school work came from a defensive attempt to preserve what they perceived as their threatened manhood. Black boys who worked hard at school were seen as 'batty men' (gay) or 'pussies' (effeminate). He emphasises that not all black boys are the same; the danger is that teachers often assume a cultural uniformity of shared values. He distinguished five categories of peer groups.

(i) Conformists
   About 41 per cent of black pupils enjoyed school and were largely conformists accepting its means and goals. To avoid having negative labels attached they dressed (even walked) differently and enjoyed a different style of music to those they knew were seen as problems.

(ii) Innovators
   About 35 per cent of Afro-Caribbean boys were categorised as 'innovators'. They accepted the goals of the school, but rejected the means. They tended to have supportive parents who encouraged them to succeed.

(iii) Retreatists
   A minority group (6 per cent) classified as 'retreatists' rejected both the goals of the school and the means of achieving success; many had special educational needs.

(iv) Hedonists
   The small numbers categorised as 'hedonists' replaced the goals and means of school with their own agenda. 'They were frequently excluded and found comfort in an anti-school black machismo.' Some white boys reported that they shared similar values and 'acted black' to be anti-school.

(v) Rebels

The group described as 'rebellious' included able pupils disaffected by clashes with particular teachers: those who were politicised and objected to the material they had to learn and which gave no pride to black people.

He concludes that schools need to:

- Examine the processes which have constructed the negative images;
- Analyse the media to see how it has exploited black male sexuality and be aware of the variations in attitudes within black groups
- Make teachers more aware of the dangers of operating with stereotypes and the ways in which peer pressures operate
- Examine the contradictory male identities that are constructed in schools.

SUMMARY

There are problems in assessing the position of members of ethnic minorities.

(i) The categories themselves are so hard to define (**Reid** says that to use classifications such as Asian and West Indian are about as useful as 'European')

(ii) Many minorities are omitted from research

(iii) Most evidence comes from small scale studies, from which it is hard to generalise.

(iv) There is some contradictory evidence to consider. On the one hand:

- Black children suffer many disadvantages, both outside and inside school.
- These appear to affect some minorities more than others and vary within them.
- Those who do underachieve are greatly over-represented in categories of the lowest streams and sets, special needs, suspension and expulsion.

On the other hand there is evidence that:

- Asian children (especially Indian) outperform their white peers (this may be more related to class than ethnic background)
- Afro-Caribbean children perform less well in primary and secondary schools
- Afro-Caribbean girls show signs of developing success strategies in school and are becoming particularly successful in higher education
- Some groups (eg the Chinese) appear to have a large section who are extremely successful and an equally large proportion who fail badly.

From a postmodern perspective there is no single theory, such as Deprivation or Cultural Difference, to explain behaviour. It is dangerous to assume that all members of a classified group are necessarily similar in their attitudes and values. The real, everyday experiences of black and white pupils in schools is not easily reducible to simple categories and statistics which have been socially constructed.

Group Work

1 List the ways group members have prejudged people, places or things and had these judgements either reinforced or changed. What were the original sources of information for the prejudgements?
2 Are teachers in any way to blame for the underachievement of black children? Assess the experiences of group members in the ways that teachers may or may not use stereotypes in their treatment of pupils, regardless of colour.

Coursework Suggestions

1 How widespread is prejudice and discrimination at the start of the twenty-first century compared to that found by Daniels and others in the 1960s and 70s?
2 Black people have contributed to the cultural heritage of Britain in many ways. Locate three who have had associations with the locality in which you study. How knowledgeable is the wider public of their contribution?

Practice Questions

1 Why might the observational methods used to obtain data about racism in education be criticised by those advocating more scientific approaches? Contrast findings from these perspectives.
2 To what extent are there variations in attainment between different black ethnic groups and between males and females? How can they be explained?
3 Evaluate the strengths and weaknesses of cultural theories to explain under-achievement in black minority groups.

10

DEBATES AND CONTROVERSIES

Introduction

THIS CHAPTER EXAMINES areas of debate which have developed around the educational system in England and Wales over the past 25 years, in particular, questions about aims and purposes of education; curriculum and its content; relationship between education and the economy; ways in which young people can be best trained, with the introduction of new vocational qualifications and the extent to which these changes may be promoting the values of a meritocratic society. Other changes in policy, the work of Ofsted and the concerns about the status and power of private and selective schools have also given rise to controversies.

Table 23: *Key Authors, Concepts and Issues in this Chapter*		
KEY AUTHORS	KEY CONCEPTS	KEY ISSUES
Marxists	Curriculum content	Areas of debate: it promotes status quo
Functionalists		It promotes an effective economy
Bayliss Dearing		Should there be training in social skills? a multicultual approach?
Bernstein	Compensatory education	Education cannot compensate for social ills
Young	Meritocracy	Occupational positions filled by the most talented
Halsey	Social mobility	An analysis of trends

Saunders	Innate ability	Is this more important than class background in determining occupational level?
Davies	Ideological policies	The effects of ideology on the 1988 Education Act
Fox Walford Roker	Private education	There has been a lack of information about the effects on girls Research about the education of girls in independent schools

IDEOLOGY AND THE CURRICULUM

The content of an educational curriculum is a matter of ideology. Policy makers decide the underlying aims, and use the curriculum to achieve them. They may be, for example, to produce an educated elite or a meritocracy; specialist technical experts or improved general standards; traditional moral and religious virtues, greater democratic values, new revolutionary attitudes or some combination of these. Marxists argue that:

- What is 'important knowledge' is what these gatekeepers of power define as important.

Functionalists argue that:

- The British educational system adapts to meet changing economic needs and these are reflected in the changes made to the curriculum from time to time. It is necessary to specify the appropriate knowledge to be learnt so that objective tests can be conducted. The most able can achieve more status.

THE CURRICULUM DEBATE

WHAT SHOULD BE IN IT?

Educationists pose the question, what is education for? What are the aims and how can these be met? What does it mean to be well educated now and what will be the requirements of a good education in the future? Traditionally, the role of the school has been seen as that of socialising children into the appropriate knowledge and values of the society. It has also emphasised the values of social control and integration. The curriculum has been used to achieve those ends.

- The 1944 Education Act specified the desire to 'revive the spiritual and personal values in our society', since religion was seen to be the 'sanctifier of human activities, the protector of group continuity, and the builder of morals and solidarity'.

- The 1988 Education Act codified existing requirements within a new framework for those aged 5–16, in the state sector and established the national curriculum (for which 70 per cent of teaching time was to be devoted). This established attainment targets which stated what children were expected to know at specified ages and emphasised the importance of the link with the economy.

Points of evaluation

- Critics argue that the national curriculum had the effect of over-centralising power with the Secretary of State for Education. For example, in 1999 David Blunkett, the Education and Employment Secretary, made his own mark on the history curriculum by advising schools that pupils over the age of eight should study the wartime exploits of the Bletchley Park code-breakers and in English, a specific list of authors.

Study point
The Conservative spokesman, David Willetts, said in response to the list (which contains authors such as Laurie Lee, Lord Byron, Dorothy Wordsworth, Gerald Durrell) that the inclusions were dangerously left wing in tone. 'It sounds as if there is a political bias in the choices, which is always the risk when people interfere in education.' What problems arise for a politician in justifying this claim?

The incoming Labour government of 1997 adopted it because it was seen as a mechanism for modernisation.

- The fact that it is a national curriculum meant that children who move schools are always at the same academic level.
- Clear guidelines are provided for teachers as to what they should be teaching.
- Parents can more easily make judgements about the effectiveness of teachers, by their results and of the school as a whole.

WHAT IS LEFT OUT?

Moral education

There is controversy as to whether the compulsory personal and social education component of the curriculum should be prescriptive in specifying appropriate moral attitudes and values, or whether these should be open to discussion and individual preference.

TO WHAT EXTENT HAS THE NATIONAL CURRICULUM INHIBITED OTHER AREAS OF SCHOOL LIFE, SUCH AS THE ARTS AND SPORT?

Training in social skills
Those who take this view argue that more consideration needs to be placed on the ways in which children are taught. There is little point in preparing people for a world in which their parents grew up. The educational curriculum of the twenty first-century requires a competence and skills-led curriculum.

Training in group creativity
The Campaign for Learning claim that to create an inclusive society and promote life-long learning, we need to convince people that education need not just mean what goes on in a formal way in school.

Training in teamwork, risk management
Those of the New right perspective express the view that the existing national curriculum should be halved, to give schools more time to develop in pupils the skills required for economic prosperity, and to develop greater individual competition amongst them.

Greater emphasis on multicultural education
The Dearing Report of 1994–5 encouraged time to be spent examining multicultural issues.

Points of Evaluation
(i)   Critics place emphasis on a need for greater cultural consensus and sense of national identity. They place more weight on the cultural heritage of Britain.

(ii) Others have said that many of the suggestions for amending the curriculum are too radical and complex. The idea of pupil-teacher negotiation would become an administative nightmare to monitor. Qualifications have to remain a benchmark of success in the pupil and the school.

(iii) Those who favour the ideas of educating for competencies note that there are such schemes under consideration in many other countries (including Scandinavia, Canada and Australia). In the School of Independent Studies, founded in Lancaster University in the 1970s, students can build up their own degree courses, if they did not like those offered in the prospectus.

Improved sex education
In the late 1990s teenage pregnancy became a major focus for policy. A government Green Paper raised the need for better sex and relationship education and more support for parents as sex educators. The national curriculum includes biological elements in Key Stages 1 and 2 and continues into 3 and 4. But there is no national data on how many schools have a sex education policy. Critics have suggested indicated that to be effective, the education has to be delivered by well trained staff, in an enlightened way and over a period of time (at least 14 hours). It also needs a more central place in the curriculum and should be an entitlement for all children from the age of four onwards.

EDUCATION AND THE ECONOMY

From a functionalist's perspective, the relationship between the economy and the educational system is a close and positive one. After the war, there was a shortage of labour and children left school at 15 with minimal qualifications, because their labour power was required. The minority who stayed on or who went to university filled the professional occupations. Later, as economic opportunities changed, the leaving age was raised to 16 and more new qualifications were introduced. This prevented too many young people flooding the labour market in the search for limited jobs. With more talented people being produced a more open society develops, with fewer barriers to mobility. Where problems remain, educational programmes to compensate them are introduced. For example, Educational Priority Areas were introduced in the 1960s–70s and in the 1990s, Education Action Zones. In the USA Operation Headstart was devised.

From a critical conflict perspective, the educational system is a microcosm of wider society, the inequalities perceived there are reflected in the organisation of schools, which stream and set largely on class lines. The result is the reproduction of the status quo. Schools produce a compliant workforce. Compensatory programmes are said to mask the real reasons for social inequalities. The schemes imply that there is something lacking in the child, rather than in the organisation of society.

Bernstein (1971) wrote: 'I cannot understand how we can talk about offering compensatory education to children who in the first place have not been offered an adequate educational environment.'

Other critics have pointed out that the high levels of illiteracy in Britain (perhaps between two and five million adults) indicate that schools are not necessarily preparing people for the world of work in a functionally useful way.

Study point

Schools serve most usefully as child minding institutions whilst mothers work, and in massaging unemployment figures, by keeping youth in school, where the tedium prepares them for their ultimate fate. There are no major job skills learnt in school. Do you agree?

Points of evaluation

(i)   The functionalist view that the educational system selects people according to their objective ability and provides them with appropriate qualifications, is based on the belief that there is a correspondence between intelligence, attainment and job achieved. This ideological perspective fits closely with that of the New Right. Policies introduced since the 1980s have ensured that testing is used; and there has been input from the free market, with new vocational qualifications.

(ii) Critics argue that the perspective largely ignores the significance and relevance of the factor of social class. The conflict theorists place much more emphasis on this issue to show how success in the marketplace is related to the social background from which the individual comes, than from any other factor. For such writers schools cannot make much difference to a fundamentally unequal society, because income and wealth as well as cultural capital are all unequally distributed. In fact, they serve to maintain the class system. Although some working-class children do succeed, this serves to perpetuate the illusion that it is a completely open society in which anyone who wishes to can reach the most prestigious social positions. The great majority are being socialised for their expected position in the workplace.

IDEOLOGY AND VOCATIONALISM

The concept of a vocation is the idea that a person has a sense of being specially suited for an occupation. Traditionally, to have a vocation in life implied a special 'calling', often into the church, or to some professional 'caring' work. The use of the term 'vocationalism' has, therefore, been imported by policy-makers to encourage school leavers to be able to move into specific areas of the economy. In 1973, the Labour government set up the Manpower Services Commission (MSC) for developing youth training, replaced in 1990 by Training and Enterprise Councils. The MSC was responsible for many innovations including:

Table 24: *Developments in Vocational Education 1978–90*

YEAR	SCHEME	DETAIL
1978	YOP	Youth Opportunity Programme A six-month programme with work experience including training in an FE college
1983	YTS	Youth Training Scheme A scheme (lasting one year, later extended to two) to provide broad-based training in a variety of Occupational areas to school leavers
1990	YT	Youth Training

The TECs (a national system of independent companies) were given the responsibility for organising and providing training in their particular locality, having examined the economic needs of the area. Subsequent Conservative governments (1979–97) introduced new qualifications based around a work-related curriculum and frameworks and relevant bodies by which to implement them. The Labour government of 1997 has added to them.

Table 25: *New Government Schemes and qualifications*

YEAR	SCHEME	DETAIL
1983	TVE1	Technical and Vocational Educational Initiative To enable 14–18 years olds to have work experience and some special courses
1985–6	CPVE	Certificate of Pre-Vocational Education For students aged over 16; provided range of work experience and practical skills
1986	NCVQ NVQ	National Council for Vocational Qualifications Aim: to introduce a system of nationally recognised vocational qualifications (NVQ) Practical achievements are rewarded by demonstrating competencies in work

1988	GCSE	General Certificate of Education This replaced the O level and CSE exam. The new qualification introduced coursework.
1994	GNVQ	General National Vocational Qualifications Aim: to allow young people to avoid early specialisation in a specific occupation. Knowledge and skills assessed in a range of different work areas, such as design leisure; catering; various services and business occupations; information technology They provide vocational-based alternatives to A levels
1995	SCAA	School Curriculum and Assessment Authority set up the National Forum for Values in Education and the Community. The 150 members published a statement of values they said should be passed from schools to children
1996	QCA	Qualifications and Curriculum Authority This body is entrusted to ensure that the standards of exams remain the same so that any changes in results can be assessed
1998	NTs	National Trainees: within a year there were 30,000 NTs. They are work-based training programmes designed by employers to train young people of 16–17 with few school qualifications to NVQ Level 2 plus other basic skills, such as IT, teamwork and numeracy

The introduction of NVQs was intended to rationalise the complicated system of vocational qualifications (there were over 300 different validating bodies). The qualifications were split into five levels, from 1, representing a foundation level, to 5, which incorporates professional qualifications. They were innovative because they did not require success in written exams. The bodies which validated them were composed mainly of industrialists (rather than educationalists) and they offered greater flexibility than previous structures. Ideologically, this fits well with the ideals of the New Right, to rekindle the entrepreneurial spirit.

Proponents of the new vocationalism argue that there had been a steady increase in the amount of job-related training between 1984 and 1994 (from 8 per cent to 14.2 per cent). Females were more likely than males to have recieved training and to have used their skills, since joining their present employer.

Points of evaluation

Critics (especially those adopting a conflict perspective) have argued that the schemes are not vocational in the sense that they answer a calling.

(i) They answer a government's need to be finding ways of occupying young people for whom A levels are not suitable examinations.

(ii) They delay the introduction of young people into the workplace who might raise unemployment figures to unacceptable levels, become politicised and join trade unions.

(iii) Evidence from Southampton University (1999) suggests that the new qualifications and options have not been fully accepted by young people as valuable. Only a third of those starting GNVQs in 1992 achieved an award by 1995.

(iv) The quality of the training received varied, yet it had to be accepted under threat of losing benefit. In 1988, entitlement to income support for most 16–17-year-old school leavers was withdrawn. The new guarantee said that all young people who were not in full time education and were between 16–18 and wished to take up YTS provision were entitled to be offered a suitable place on the programme. By 1995 there were more than 50,000 school leavers who were not receiving training and were without income support.

MERITOCRACY

The concept of meritocracy came into sociological usage in 1958 when **Young** described a time in the future when all occupational status positions would be filled on the basis of talent. He warned that this could lead to social antagonisms, as those excluded from positions of power became increasingly resentful and opposed to those who did. If every position in work is obtained on merit then:

- Those who achieve greatest power do so because they can demonstrate that they have more ability (judged by qualifications, and other factors associated with the requirements of the job) than their competitors.
- Issues of heredity, family background, wealth and network connections, would not be relevant in the appointment of someone to a post.
- The democratic ideology and the meritocratic principle justifies the use of exams, tests and other tools of assessment to establish those with the best skills for the occupational requirements.

Halsey (1980) argues, from a liberal perspective, that educational reforms can change society and promote greater upward mobility and produce a more meritocratic society. Although in *Origins and Destinations*, he concedes that by that time middle class children had obtained more benefits from the changes to the structure of the educational system than working class children, he was hopeful that this would not continue to be the case. However, by 1990–1, only 3 per cent of men and 1 per cent of women from unskilled working class backgrounds were attending universities.

Points of evaluation

- The question remains as to how merit is established or assessed. Middle class children hold greater cultural capital in terms of social and linguistic skills; as a result, even able and enthusiastic working class children fail to obtain high status positions, whereas the less competent middle class children frequently do.

- IQ tests have been shown to be open to major criticism and their results of dubious value in assessing innate talent. There remain many inequalities in the control of the most powerful institutions, where school and family background may still be influential, rather than talent.

- Many very able and talented people end up in low status occupations even though their credentials are identical to the successful candidate.

On this argument, Britain is not meritocratic, despite the changes in the educational structure.

Proponents of the concept of meritocracy point out that one of the major objectives of the reforms which have been undertaken in the British educational system since 1944 has been based on the relatively successful aim of creating a more meritocratic system through the provision of greater educational opportunities.

- More women are breaking through the 'glass ceiling' which has traditionally limited their opportunities.

- Ethnic minorities are also benefiting as increasing numbers achieve high levels of academic and occupational success.

- The question of the validity of IQ tests and their relationship to social class has been reconsidered by **Saunders** (1996). He concludes that whilst class origins have some effect on success in life, more important is ability, which has been undervalued as an explanation by sociologists.

- There has been a steady increase in the number of working class pupils reaching university.

Saunders says 'Britain is not yet a genuine meritocracy, but is much closer to being one than many people realise'.

OFFICE FOR STANDARDS IN EDUCATION

Ofsted began its work in 1992/3. Its first annual report appeared in 1993/4. A team of inspectors has the duty of grading the lessons they observe as well as the quality and efficiency of the schools. From this data, year-on-year comparisons are made and league tables drawn up and published from which government policy may be formulated. For example, a suggestion from Ofsted that smaller class sizes for children 8–11 years old had no effect on results justified a maximum class size of 30. The finding (in *Primary Education: A Review of Primary Schools in England 1994–98*) that whole class teaching is more effective than group work has ensured that this becomes more widely used.

Ofsted inspectors have:

- Put more than 850 schools on 'special measures' between 1993 and 1999. About 80 of these were subsequently closed; a further 291 were successful in improving their standards, and judged to provide an acceptable education for their pupils.
- Told schools to celebrate their pupil's achievements, raise their self-esteem, promote positive attitudes and find ways of limiting truancy.
- Insisted that teachers improve their skills, with good schemes of work.
- Informed headteachers to provide dynamic leadership.
- Revealed at least 15,000 incompetent teachers.
- Reported in 1999 that 50% of lessons taught to 7–11 year olds are routinely judged to be good.'

In 1994–5 less than 40 per cent of schools were teaching English and maths well or very well. Reading was generally better taught than writing which was relatively neglected. It paid tribute to an improvement in teachers' knowledge, skills and understanding of the subjects they teach. But 25 per cent of schools remained bad at teaching information technology. One in eight headteachers were failing to lead their schools effectively. The policy of 'naming and shaming' those schools whose standards were unacceptably low was advocated.

Points of evaluation

(i) The outcome of the testing procedures is that schools can be placed in league tables showing relative levels of success. However, one outcome which has been criticised is that the testing has resulted in children becoming assessed rather than the school. They know how their classmates have done and make their own comparisons. This can result in lowering their self esteem, especially when they attend a secondary school which uses the results to stream the new intakes.

(ii) Whilst Ofsted supporters claim that strict inspection routines have assisted in the raising of standards, critics note that they have also risen in Scotland and Northern Ireland, where it has no role. In England and Wales improvements in exam results for 16 year olds actually began to rise in 1980. This suggests other factors influencing results such as economic ones.

(iii) Critics of Ofsted argue that there should be more concern for teacher morale. A committee of MPs suggested in 1999 that there should be a supervisory board to oversee Ofsted's performance.

LITERACY AND NUMERACY

In 1998 the proportion of 11 year olds passing the expected standard in maths fell from 62 per cent to 59 per cent. In English, it rose by 2 per cent to 65 per cent. However, in 1999 pupils achieved even better results in their SATs tests. A Literacy Hour was introduced into primary schools in 1998. In 1999 the government launched a national initiative to improve standards of literacy and numeracy with all people, both children and adult learners. The year 2000 was designated Numeracy Year to encourage parents and the wider community to interest children in arithmetic. The target of ensuring that 80 per cent of 11 year olds would reach specific literacy standards by 2002 was set.

The outcome of GCSE results in 1999 showed:

- A resurgence of traditional subjects in the examinations.
- Evidence of 18 year olds switching to more vocational A level subjects
- An increase in numbers taking English literature, physics, chemistry and biology.
- The most popular subject continued to be maths (625,950 entries) and English (501,951 entries).
- About 46 per cent of the candidates gained 5 or more passes at Grade C or above. The Government aimed is to increase this to 50 per cent by 2002.
- A 70 per cent increase in the number of entries for the experimental part one GNVQs which are intended to offer an applied alternative to GCSEs (17,459 candidates).
- 20 per cent of pupils left school without a Grade G in English or maths and 6 per cent had no qualifications.

SELECTION

The belief that schools should be able to select their pupils by means of special tests is a feature of Conservative ideological belief. The principle of comprehensive education, by which all children in a locality attend the same school without test, is part of Labour or socialist ideology. The move towards comprehensivisation started in 1947 and developed more strongly after 1964 when Labour next came to power. This also marked the decline, but not the end of the grammar school system. They cannot co-exist alongside comprehensive schools. However, they were retained in areas where the Conservative councils were able to control the structure of local education.

Lord Baker, the Secretary of State for Education in the 1980s, introduced policies to inhibit the growth of comprehensive schools. These were designed to undermine the teaching unions, to kill off local education authorities and to wipe out comprehensive schools by stealth. He confirms in an interview with **Davies** (*Guardian* 16 September 1999) that the reforms were not based on solid research but on 'guesswork, personal whim and bare knuckle politics.' Davies concludes that 'on the basis of his personal experience, he built his policy.'

THE 1988 ACT:

(i) This introduced Local Management of Schools (LMS) by which heads controlled the entire budget for their schools, rather than leaving it in the hands of the LEA. The effect was also to fragment the unions, by giving them thousands of different employers to deal with and limiting the chances of collective bargaining.

(ii) It provided parents with the right to choose their child's school. This was achieved by setting minimum admission numbers for each school. It was Baker's agenda to make both the LEAs and the comprehensive schools 'wither on the vine'. Some schools expanded and quickly filled their places because they were favoured. These attracted the most funds. Others lost support and because places were vacant, were obliged to fill them with children who had been excluded or who could not get into their first choice schools. Inevitably their examination results were less good, and their reputation was further diminished. Funds were also cut.

(iii) It established City Technology Colleges and Grant-Maintained schools, which increased parental choice. He was thereby reasserting a selective system in which the schools most highly regarded became the equivalent of the grammar schools and those which were rejected were the equivalent of the old secondary modern schools, and stigmatised as 'less successful' and so with smaller numbers operate on reduced budgets.

The Labour government of 1997 was committed to a policy of no selection by examination or interview. They claimed that they would leave the future of grammar schools to be decided by a ballot of 'all affected parents' as a form of local democracy. To trigger a vote, at least 20 per cent of parents in an area in which a grammar school exists must support the petition to change the status of the school and their entry criteria.

In 1999 secondary headteachers called on the government to investigate the use of covert selection methods by some comprehensive schools to enroll the most able pupils and so improve their exam results and thereby attract more funds and even better pupils. Some comprehensives were adopting testing procedures for the Year 6 pupils in local primary schools, to allocate places. However, it remained Labour policy to allow a comprehensive school to select up to 15 per cent of intake by ability.

Points of evaluation

Proponents of Grammar Schools argue that they are a means of achieving upward mobility for clever working class children. Critics of the selection process note that statistics published in 1999 showed that in some areas less than 1 per cent of grammar school pupils were eligible for free school meals, the most commonly used indicator of poverty. In every part of the country grammar schools have fewer than the average for their area. This suggests that the idea that this is an escape route for children from low income families, is mistaken.

EDUCATION AND PRIVATE SCHOOLS

IS THERE STILL A ROLE FOR INDEPENDENT SCHOOLS?

The highest fee paying schools, the elite are known as Public Schools. There are 233 whose heads attend the Headmaster's Conference (HC) to which they are affiliated and whose traditional aims, since being founded in 1871, were to combat any political attacks made on them and prepare their pupils for public office. However, there are just over 2,000 registered private schools which educate about 600,000 children (approximately 7.5 per cent of the school population 5–16). The figure increases to about 19 per cent at 16+ . These schools are not maintained by the state and not subject to Ofsted inspections or the requirements of the national curriculum, although they do have to conform to certain required regulations regarding facilities. They are financed through fees, gifts and bequests.

These HC schools have traditionally produced more members of powerful interest, business and political groups. Proponents point to their smaller classes, excellent facilities, especially for sport, and high academic standards. Their critics argue that they:

- Provide special advantages, often maintaining unfair links with Oxbridge and an effective old school tie network (Although in 1999, for the first time, the number of offers made by Oxford to candidates from the state sector exceeded those from the independents.)
- Maintain existing inequalities in the social structure. They are not community oriented in that they do not attract pupils from a local area.
- Staff are not always properly qualified.

Table 26: *The top independent schools at A level (A=10 points, B=8 etc)*

SCHOOL	NO. OF CANDIDATES	AVERAGE	FEES, P.A.
Winchester	134	34	£16,110
St Paul's London	160	32.8	£14,910
Westminster School, London	162	32.7	£16,068
Sevenoaks	97	31.4	£15,213
Twycross House, Athersone	17	31	£4,290

Table 27: *The top schools for GCSE rsults were based on A=8, G=1*

SCHOOL	NO. OF CANDIDATES	AVERAGE	FEES, P.A.
Abbey Girls School (Reading)	101	77.77	£5,100
King Edward 6th Girls High School	74	77.51	£5,385
St Paul's School (London)	149	77.3	£14,910
King Edward's School (Bgh'm)	125	76.88	£5,523
Perse School for Girls	85	76.48	£5,862

Source: Guardian 1999

The educational background of judges is an example of the influence of a public school in maintaining its hold on top jobs. A survey published in 1999 by *Labour Research* magazine showed that two years after Labour took office judges on the circuit bench and above wre as overwhelmingly white, male and public school educated as ever, despite the fact that most judicial posts were advertised, there has been an attempt to encourage women and ethnic minorities to apply. Since 1997:

- Of 85 judges appointed seven were women.
- Fewer than 1 per cent of judges (none at High Court level or above) were from ethnic minorities
- 8 out of 10 judges (79 per cent) appointed or promoted were educated at public schools (compared with 69 per cent of all judges and 84 per cent of High Court judges)
- Of the present judges, Eton provided 20; Winchester 14
- 73 per cent of judges appointed or promoted since 1997 had been educated at Oxbridge (compared to an overall average of 64 per cent).

By 1992 two thirds of the HC (which had been forced to change its policy of excluding schools that accepted girls) were co-educational. This may have been a factor in the improving educational standards recorded for such schools.

Fox (1989) noted that at that time there were virtually no details about girls in the private sector. A few studies have been undertaken since that time.

Walford (1990) notes that about 20 per cent of girls are in HC schools. There are 240 schools in the Governing Bodies of Girls Schools Association (GBGSA) which has a wider range of size, geographical location and religious affiliation. The proportion of girls being educated privately has increased more rapidly than boys in HC schools. Over 400 private schools educate girls only.

Roker (1994) investigated these issues. She agrees that there are significant differences in the outcomes of the educational processes for girls in different types of educational institution. Those in private schools appeared to have limited experience of unemployment problems or those of poverty; whereas those in state schools had a wider view of social life. Their social contacts were with girls of similar social background and from within the school; few indicated that they might support the Labour Party in an election. There was little political discussion, because there was so much general agreement. On the other hand, the girls showed a more singular set of aims; A levels, university and professional career. They appeared more competitive and assertive.

The preparatory school (which feeds the independents) is for pupils aged 3–13 and educates more than 124,000 pupils of whom more than 12,000 are borders. A survey in 1999 showed that 55 per cent offer care before school starts (in the form of a breakfast club) and 85 per cent offer after school care. Almost all teach French; 66 per cent teach Latin and 16 per cent Greek. The average fee was £1,874 per term (£3,310 for borders). Average class size 15. They have been found to teach on average 100 hours longer than the recommended minimum for state primaries.

Points of evaluation
Those who defend the private sector argue that:

(i)   They provide a range of alternative types of schools from which parents can choose to educate their children.

(ii) There are also other types in the private sector which provide specialist education, including those for music, evangelical Christianity and Muslims. Consequently, they do not all provide exclusive routes to positions of power and authority.

(iii) There is not sufficient evidence to show a direct link between private education and examination and occupational success. The superior results of private schools is due to their selection process, whereby they cream off the ablest children, in the way that grammar schools used to do.

The critics of the private sector point out that:

(i)   They have produced people who may have been good administrators, but they did not encourage a modernising, scientific outlook which would produce an effective modern economy. The result was a long term industrial malaise in the manufacturing sector.

(ii) They promote a set of conservative values in society which:

- Inhibit the development of a healthy meritocratic, community oriented society
- Encourage attitudes of deference to the aristocratic and elite sector of society.

However, the Labour Party which has traditionally opposed their existence has not proposed their total abolition, since they are such well established institutions and the outcomes could be politically and socially uncertain. Some senior party members make use of them for their children.

THE PROFESSIONALISATION OF TEACHERS

By a profession, sociologists mean that the occupation has certain characteristics. These include:

- High social status for members, because it is difficult to enter and is usually well paid (for example medicine, dentistry, the law)
- High levels of qualification because members must develop specialised knowledge of which the lay person is largely ignorant
- A special code of ethics which controls the behaviour of the members (such as rules governing relationships between clients and practitioner)
- A special culture and members sometimes wear special clothes (such as a wig or gown)
- A controlling body which supervises their activities, regulates and officially registers and disciplines them (such as the Law Society).

The position of the teacher has been that of a semi-profession, in that some of the characteristics of the typical professional were met, but not all. They have been unionised, but have never had a professional association. From 1 September 2000 the General Teaching Council takes on this role. The Director can register and strike off state school teachers. The new body is an equivalent of the General Medical Council for doctors. It has a dual role in regulating and promoting the teaching profession. It also advises the Secretary of State, LEAs and the schools themselves on the recruitment, supply and registration of teachers, their training and further professional development. In 1999 the government introduced performance incentives to include additional payments of £2,000 for experienced teachers who had reached the classroom pay maximum. The aim was to further develop levels of professionalism among teachers, which unions argued had been undermined by moves to curb the autonomy of teachers by the educational changes of the 1980s, under conservative administrations.

SUMMARY

There is no universally agreed definition of education or its true goals. These are shaped by changing ideologies of the political parties which implement policies. Consequently, these are subject to constant debate and controversy. The Education Act of 1988 introduced major reforms, advocated by the New Right, including the national curriculum, a new emphasis on vocational education and inspection teams (Ofsted) to monitor standards. Other areas of concern have been in relation to selection and the place of independent schools.

Coursework Suggestions

1 Does private education have a future? Assess the attitudes of a random sample.
2 The new vocationalism: how well informed are a sample of the public about the changes over the past 10 years? What value do they place on the range of qualifications? Should more be done to publicise them?

Practice Questions

1 Assess sociological explanations of the role and significance of private education in contemporary Britain.
2 To what extent are all policy makers, of both main parties, influenced by the view that the function of education is to ensure economic well being, rather than a more equal society?
3 Will the new vocationalism produce a more meritocratic society?

SUGGESTED READING

EDUCATION AND IDEOLOGY

Thompson, K. *Beliefs and Ideology* (1986) Ellis Horwood and Tavistock Publications
Halsey, A. *Change in British Society* (1986) Oxford University Press
Erikson, K. *Wayward Puritan* (1966) Wiley
Usher, R. and Edwards, R. *Postmodernism and Education* (1994) Routledge
Crossland, A. *The Future of Socialism* (1981) Cape
Chitty, C. *Sociology Review* (1993) Vol 2 No 3 and (1997) Vol 6 No 4
Demaine, J. *Education Policy and Contemporary Politics* (1999) Routledge

FUNCTIONALIST THEORIES OF EDUCATION

Durkheim, E. *Education and Society* (1956) Free Press.
Parsons, T. and Bales, R. *Family, Socialisation and Interaction Processes* (1968) Routledge
Ricks, F. and Pryke, S. 'Teacher perceptions and attitudes'. (1973) *Interchange* Vol 4 No 1

CONFLICT THEORIES OF EDUCATION

Marx, K. see Worsley, P. *Marx and Marxism* (1982) Horwood and Tavistock
Bowles, S. and Gintis, H. *Schooling in Capitalist America* (1976)
Bordieu, P. 'Cultural reproduction and social reproduction' (1973) in Brown, R. (ed) *Knowledge, Education and Cultural Change*, Tavistock
Althusser, L. 'Ideology and ideological state apparatuses' (1972) in Cosin, B. (ed) *Education, Structure and Society*, Penguin
Sharp, R. and Green, A. *Education and Social Control* (1975) Routledge
Willis, P. *Learning to Labour* (1977) Saxon House
Milliband, R. *Divided Societies* (1991) Oxford Paperbacks
Reeves, F. *Further Education as Economic Regeneration* (1997) Bilston College Publications and Education Now
Measor, L. and Sikes, P. *Gender and Schools* (1992) Cassell

INTERPRETATIVE PERSPECTIVES OF EDUCATION

Mead, G. *Mind Self and Society* (1934) University of Chicago Press
Blumer, H. *Symbolic Interactionism* (1969) Prentice-Hall
Goffman, E. *The Presentation of Self in Everyday Life* (1959) Penguin
Becker, H. *Labelling Theory Re-considered* in Rock, P. and MacIntosh, M. (1974) Tavistock
Rist, R. 'On understanding the processes of schooling' (1977) in Karabel and Halsey *Power and Ideology in Education*, Oxford University Press
Keddie, N. 'Classroom knowledge' (1971) in Young, M. *Knowledge and Control*, Collier-Macmillan
Good, T. and Brophey J. *Looking in Classrooms* (1978) Harper Row
Meighan, R. et al *Perspectives on Society* (1979) Thomas Nelson
Mirza, H. 'Black female success' (1997) *Social Science Teacher* Vol 26 No3

CONTEMPORARY APPROACHES IN EDUCATION

Hulme, M. 'Resisting perspectivitis' (1999) *Social Science Teacher* No 3 Summer

Habermas, J. *Legitimation Crisis* (1976) Heinemann

Davies, B. *Frogs and Snails and Feminists Tales* (1989) Allen and Unwin

Layder, D. and Clarke, J. 'Let's get real' (1994) *Sociology Review* Vol 4 No 2

Usher, R. and Edwards, R. *Postmodernism and Education* (1994) Routledge

Giddens, A. *The Consequences of Modernity* (1990) Polity Press

Elliott, J. and Adelman, C. *Innovation at the Classroom Level* (1976) Open University Educational Enterprises

Mortimer, et al *School Matters: the Junior Years* (1988) Open Books

Cockett, M. and Tripp, J. *Children Living in Re-ordered Families* (1994) Rowntree Trust

Quicke, J. 'Personal and social education' (1986) *Educational Review* Vol 38 No 3

Gillborn, D. *Race, Ethnicity and Education* (1990) Unwin Hyman

Herrnstein, R. and Murray, C. *The Bell Curve: Intelligence and Class Structure in American Life* (1994) Free Press

Mevarech, M. et al 'Is more always better?' (1992) *British Journal of Educational Psychology* 62

FACTORS AFFECTING EDUCATIONAL PERFORMANCE

Willmott, P. and Young, M. *Family and Kinship in East London* (1957) Routledge

Douglas, J. W. et al *All Our Future* (1971) Panther

Westergaard, J. 'class today: fashions at Odds with facts' (1996) *Social Science Teacher* Vol 25 No 2

Reid, I. 'Education and inequality' (1996) *Sociology Review* Vol 6 No 2

Wedge, P. and Prosser, H. *Born to Fail?* (1973) Arrow Books

Lockwood, D. and Goldwood, J. 'Affluence and the British Class Structure' (1963) *Sociological Review* Vol 11 No 2

Bourdieu, P. 'The school as a conservative force (1974) in Egglestone J. *Contemporary Research in the Sociology of Education*, Methuen

Bernstein, B. *Class Codes and Control* Vol 3 (1977) Routledge

Rosen, H. *Language and Class* (1974) Falling Wall Press

Labov, W. 'The logic of nonstandard English' (1973) in Keddie, N. *Tinker Tailor:. The Myth of Cultural Deprivation*, Penguin

Milson, F. *Youth in a Changing Society* (1972) Routledge

Hargreaves, D. et al *Deviance in Classrooms* (1975) Routledge

Rosenthal, R. and Jacobson, L. *Pygmalion in the Classoom* (1968) Holt

Lemert, E. *Human Deviance, Social Problems and Social Control* (1972) Prentice-Hall

Reynolds, D. 'The delinquent school' (1976) in Woods, P. *The Process of Schooling*, Routledge

Reynolds, D. 'School effectiveness, school improvement and contemporary educational policies' (1999) in Demaine, J. *Education, Policy and Contemporary Politics*, Macmillan

Thomas et al 'Determining what adds value to student achievement' (1995) *Education Leadership International* Vol 58 No 6

Sammons, P. et al 'Differential School Effectiveness' (1993) *British Educational Research Journal* Vol 19 No 4

Daly, P. *How Large are Secondary School Effects in Northern Ireland?* (1991) School Effectiveness and School Improvement

Brown, S. et al 'Possibilities and problems of small scale studies' (1996) in Gray et al *Merging Traditions* , Cassell

Reynolds, D. 'The effective school' (1996) *Evaluation and Research in Education* Vol 9 No 2

Hutchinson, B. and Whitehouse, P. 'Action research, professional competence and school organisation (1986) *British Educational Research Journal* Vol 12 No 1

Hammersley, M. and Turner, G. (1984) 'Conformist pupils' in Hammersley, M. and Woods, P. *Life in School, the Sociology of Pupil Culture*, Open University Press

Hopkins, D. *A Teacher's Guide to Classroom Research* (1996) Open University Press

Slavin, R. *Education for All* (1996) Lisse: Swets and Zeitlinger

Blishen, E. *The School That I'd Like* (1969) Penguin

Veldman, D. and Peck, R. 'Student teacher characteristics from the pupil's viewpoint' (1963) *Journal of Educational Psychology* 54

Brake, M. *Comparative Youth Subcultures* (1985) Routledge

Hebdige, D. *Subculture: The Meaning of Style* (1979) Methuen

GENDER AND EDUCATION

Abbott, P. and Wallace, C. *An Introduction to Sociology: Feminist Perspectives* (1997) Routledge

Barber, M. *Young People and their Attitudes to School* (1994) Keele University

Epstein, D. et al *Failing Boys* Open University Press

Equal Opportunities Commission (EOC) *Briefings on Women and Men in Britain* (1966) HMSO

Greer, G. *Female Eunoch* (1971) Paladin

Hakim, C. *The Sexual Division of Labour and Women's Heterogeneity* (1996) BJS Vol 47 No 1

Kamin, 'Behind the curve' (1995) *Scientific American* February

Meighan, R. *A Sociology of Educating* (1981) Holt

Millett, K. *Sexual Politics* (1970) Doubleday

Oakley, A. *Housewife* (1974) Allan Lane

Phillips, A. *The Trouble With Boys* (1993) Pandora

Pilcher, J. 'Hormones or hegemonic masculinity' *Sociology Review* Vol 7 No 3

Reid, I. 'Education and inequality' (1996) *Sociology Review* Vol 6 No 2

Ridell, S. *Gender and the Politics of the Curriculum* (1992) Routledge

Sharpe, S. *Just Like a Girl* (1994) Penguin

Spender, D. *Invisible Women: Schooling Scandal* (1983) Women's Press

Walby, S. *Theorising Patriarchy* (1990) Blackwell

Whitelegg, E. *The Changing Experience of Women* (1982) Martin Robertson and OU

ETHNICITY AND EDUCATION

Rex, J. and Tomlinson, S. *Colonial Immigrants in a British City* (1979) Routledge

Swann Report *Education for All* (1985) HMSO

Rutter, M. et al 'Children and West Indian immigrants' (1974) *New Society* March 14

Clarke, J. 'Ethnicity and education re-visited' (1997) *Sociology Review* Vol 7 No 2

Kysel, F. 'Ethnic background and examination results' (1988) *Educational Research* Vol 30 No2

Modood, T. and Shiner, M. *Ethnic Minorities and Higher Education* (1994) PSI Report

Jones, T. *Britain's Ethnic Minorities* (1993) PSI

Mabey, C. *Black Pupils' Achievement in Inner London* (1986) Educational Research Vol 28 No 3

MacKay, T. 'Education and the disadvantaged' (1999) *The Psychologist* Vol 12 No 7

Office of Population Censuses and Surverys (OPCS) (1991) HMSO

Whitmarsh, A. and Summerfield, C. *Social Focus on Ethnic Minorities* (1996) Office for National Statistics, HMSO

Cole, T. *Wealth Poverty and Welfare* (1999) Hodder & Stoughton

Drew, D. et al 'Ethnic differences in the educational participation of 16–19 year olds' (1997) in Karn, V. *Ethnicity in the 1991 Census* Vol 4 HMSO

Drew, D. and Gray, J. 'The fifth year examination achievements of black young people in England and Wales' (1990) *Educational Research* Vol 32 No 2

Daniel, W. *Racial Discrimination in England and Wales* (1966) Penguin

McIntosh, N. and Smith, D. *The Extent of Racial Discrimination* (1966) HMSO

PSI Reports *Black and White Britain* (1984; 1997) HMSO

Lewis, R. *Anti-Racism: A Mania Exposed* (1988) Quartet Books

Commission for Racial Equality Report *Ethnic Minority Schoolteachers* (1988) HMSO

Wright, C. *Race Relations in the Primary School* (1992) Fulton

Connolly, P. and Troyna, B. *Researching Racism in Education* (1998) Open University Press

Gillborn, D. *Race, Ethnicity and Education* (1990) Unwin Hyman

Foster, P. et al *Constructing Educational Inequality* (1996) Falmer

Cross, W. 'Black identity' (1985) in Spencer, M. et al *The Social and Affective Development of Black Children*, Erlbaum

Policy Studies Institute Report *Ethnic Minorities* (1997) HMSO

Armenta Marketing *The Black Child Report* (1997)

Bhatti, G. *Asian Children at Home and At School* (1999) Routledge

Fleming, S. 'Schooling, sport and ethnicity' (1993) *Sociology Review* Vol 3 No 1

Jaggi, M. *Black British Culture and Society* (1999) Routledge

Bulmer, M. and Solomos, J. *Ethnic and Racial Studies Today* (1999) Routledge

Wright, C. 'School processes, an ethnographic study' (1987) in Eggleston, J. et al *Education for Some*, Trentham Books

Gillborn, D. 'Racism and the politics of qualitative research: learning from controversy and critique' (1999) in Connolly, P and Troyna, B. *Researching Racism in Education*, Open University Press

Foster, P. *Policy and Practice* (1990) Routledge

Smith, D. and Tomlinson, S. *The School Effects* (1989) Policy Studies Institute

Woods, P. *The Happiest Days: How Pupils Cope With School* (1990) Falmer

Ofsted Reports (1993–4) HMSO

Employment Gazette (1993/1995) HMSO

DEBATES AND CONTROVERSIES

Bernstein, B. 'Education cannot compensate for society' (1971) in Cosin, B et al *School and Society*, Routledge

Young, M. *The Rise of the Meritocracy* (1958) Thames and Hudson

Halsey, A. et al *Origins and Destinations* (1980) Clarendon Press

Saunders, P. 'The Bell Curve' (1996) *Sociology Review* Vol 6 No 2

Ofsted Report *Primary Education: A Review of Primary Schools in England 1994—1998* HMSO

Davies, N. *Guardian* 16 September 1999

Fox, I. 'Elitism and British Public Schools' (1989) in Cibulka, J. et al *Private Schools and Public Policy*, Falmer

Walford, G. *The Private Schooling of Girls: Past and Present* (1993) Frank Cass

Roker, D. 'Girls in private schools' (1994) *Sociology Review* Vol 4 No 2

USEFUL WEBSITES

ESRC Teaching and Learning Research
Programme
www.ex.ac.uk/ESRC-TLRP

British towards 2010
www.esrc.ac.uk/2010/docs/britain.html

Guardian's education information
www.educationunlimited.co.uk
This provides an archive of all the articles from
the paper, special reports on key educational
issues, an exlusive directory of recommended
sites for teachers and an online forum for ideas
and projects

Journal storage; web-based archival backfile
service
www.csupomna.edu/~library/html/jsy.or.html

Education Action Zones
www.dfee.gov.uk/easz

Pupil mobility in schools
www.dfee.gove.uk/education/

Teacher awards
infro@teachingawards.com(020-7388 1911)
www.teaching awards.co

Government's National Grid for Learning
This provides annotated links to many
curriculum sites
www.ngfl.gov.uk

Group to encourage ethnic minority students
at Cambridge
www.cam.ac.uk/CambUni/BapProsepctus/
geema.html

For advice on what to do on leaving
university
www.thebigtrip.co.uk

British Association for Counselling
www.counselling.co.uk

Information on remarking of exams
www.edexcel.org.uk

Appeals procedures
www.aeb.org.uk

Ofsted reports
www.ofsted.gov.uk/parents/maintenance/
i2.thm
www.schools-net.com

For league tables (also under performance
tables)
www.dfee.gov.uk

National curriculum
www.nc.uk.net

BBCs Learning Zone
www.bbc.co.uk/education/directory/

Learning Resources online
www.bbc.co.uk/schools

Open University
open.ac.uk

Ingenta
www.ingenta.com
Gives access to over 750,000 articles from 2,300
academic journals.

Teacher-training website
www.teach.tta.gov.uk

Association for Teaching Social Science
www.le.ac.uk/education/centre/ATSS/atss.h
tml

Social Science Information Gateway
www.sosig.esrc.bris.ac.uk/

Sociology Department (Lancaster University)
www.comp.lanc.ac.uk/sociology/respaper.html
For publication of texts destined to become
books, chapters or articles.

A general site which will lead to other useful
areas
www.yahoo.com/social-science/sociology/

INDEX